The Grammar of Cooking

The Grammar of
COOKING

CAROL BRAIDER

CHESTATEE REGIONAL LIBRARY
GAINESVILLE, GEORGIA 30501

Holt, Rinehart and Winston
New York, Chicago, San Francisco

Copyright © 1974 by Carol Braider

All rights reserved, including the right to reproduce this book or portions thereof in any form.

Published simultaneously in Canada by Holt, Rinehart and Winston of Canada, Limited.

Library of Congress Cataloging in Publication Data
Braider, Carol.
  The grammar of cooking.
  Bibliography: p.
  1. Cookery. I. Title.
TX651.B68   641.5   73-3743
ISBN 0-03-010726-1

First Edition

Designer: James McCrea

Printed in the United States of America

For my family: Donald, Susan, Jackson, Christopher, and Helen . . . and for those dear friends who have sat at our table and, thus, made this book seem possible . . . with my love.

Contents

    A Prefatory Note   xi
    Introduction   xiii

1. A Simple Subject: Roasting, Broiling, Pan-broiling, Spit-Roasting   3
    Roasting   13
    Broiling   26
    Panbroiling   32
    Spit-Roasting   33

2. Compound Subjects: Deep Frying, Panfrying, Sautéing   37
    Deep Frying   38
    Panfrying and Sautéing   43

3. The Adjectival Clause: Stocks, *Courts Bouillons, Fumets*   49
    Stocks   49
    Courts Bouillons   57

Fumets 58
Meager Stocks (Stocks Made with Leftovers) 58

4. The Run-on Sentence: Cooking in Liquids 60
   Steaming 62
   Boiling 63
   Stewing 66
   Poaching 70

5. Modifiers: Preparations for Combination and Sauce Cookery 72
   Larding 73
   Marinating 73
   Blanching 75
   Mirepoix 76
   Matignon 77
   Roux 78
   Beurre Manié 80

6. The Compound Sentence: Combination Cooking 81
   Braising 84
   Pot Roasting 91
   Fricasseeing 92
   À la Poêle 93
   En Casserole and *en Cocotte* 94
   Au Gratin 95
   Glazing 95
   Forcemeats: Meat Loaf, Pâté, and Sausage 96

7. The Pluperfect: The Egg and Its Special Dishes 99
   Mastering the Egg 100
   Magic with Eggs 105
   Egg Cookery 109
   Eggs in Combination with Other Ingredients 114

8. The Imperative: Soups   117
   Soups   119
   Types of Soups   122

9. Qualifying Phrases: Sauces, the Consummate Achievement of Cooking   127
   Sauces: Homogeneous and Contrasting   128
   Types of Sauces   132
   Compound Sauces   139

10. Punctuation: Herbs and Spices, Salts, Sweeteners   142
    Basic Herbs   144
    Basic Spices   146
    Salts   148
    Acids: Vinegars   149
    Hot Seasonings   149
    Pungents   150
    Hot Condiments   150
    Sweeteners   150

11. The Complementary Phrase: Baking   151
    Baking Cakes   153
    Preparing Pastry   158
    Making Cookies   160

12. The Indispensable Predicate: Vegetables, Starches, and Fruits   161
    Vegetables   162
    Starches: Grains, Pasta, Rice, Beans, Peas, Lentils, and Chickpeas   176
    Fruits   177

13. Parsing: How to Read a Recipe   180
    Reading a Recipe   182

14. Rhyming: Menu Planning and Serving Suggestions 188
    Menu Planning   190
    Serving Suggestions   194

Appendices
  I. Weights and Measures in the United States and Great Britain   201
  II. Kitchen Equipment   205
  III. An Opinionated Bibliography   213
      Index   217

A Prefatory Note

I call this book *The Grammar of Cooking* not because I am a grammarian (my husband supplied that expertise), but because I wanted to implant in the reader's mind a particular kind of conception: Cooking is a construction process, and so I used an analogy with which we are all—whether consciously or not—familiar, the construction of sentences.

We speak and write with letters and words, thus forming sentences, paragraphs, chapters, books. So it is with cooking —a putting together of elements, most of them simple, to make dishes and whole menus.

If *I* were to compose a linguistic grammar, I should begin by comparing language to cooking. You take a few raw products, words, and begin to build.

It's customary and only proper to acknowledge the debt one owes for the making of a book . . . in this case, my editor and dear friend, Pace Barnes, whose idea it was. I'm sure Pace would agree that it wouldn't have seen the light of day without the support and writer's craft of my husband, Donald.

C.B.

Clinton, New York
January 1974

Introduction

Discovering the Mystery of Good Food

In 1932, when I was only six, my parents took my three older sisters and me for a prolonged tour of Western Europe, with the heaviest emphasis—at least so far as *I* was concerned—on France. At the time of our departure I couldn't know, of course, that this was to be the beginning of an adventure that has yet to end. It is one, indeed, with which I am more deeply involved and to which I am more profoundly committed today than I was in that childhood year. For it was in France that I made the discovery that food could be prepared in ways that were exciting, not merely edible. It was in France, as I approached the age of seven, that I was accorded culinary revelation—in the manner of Saint Paul on the road to Damascus.

My boundless curiosity about the taste of food allowed me to introduce myself to oysters at Etretat and to mussels at La Boule. I ate my first *crêpes Suzette* at Beaulieu, on the Mediterranean. The childish joy I felt as I watched the waiter preparing the *crêpes* on the serving table beside me has endured. It has become traditional for me to offer *crêpes Suzette* every New Year's Eve for family and friends. We have always celebrated this occasion with lots of food accompanied by a modicum of drink—eschewing the more common custom of reversing the order of things.

I shall not enumerate all the simple or exotic dishes that I savored for the first time during our ten-month stay abroad in 1932. The point is that the experience genuinely transfigured me. Even to write of that period evokes pangs of nostalgia and hunger in approximately equal proportion, and reminds me that my passion for food and for the discovery of new and pleasant ways to prepare it has persisted with the constancy of a faithful dog. It is still transfiguring me—in more ways than one, alas!

Discovering the Mystery of Preparation

Following our return to the United States, I began to nag my mother to allow me to try to cook something myself. I still don't understand why she resisted my stubbornly repeated entreaties for so long—unless the explanation is that she didn't want the regime of her well-staffed kitchen to be disturbed. However, when it was plain that I was absolutely determined to learn, she finally gave way.

One summer's morning, to my ecstatic delight, she told me to ask Mary, our cook, to give me certain cookbooks from which Mother would select a recipe which *she* thought suitable for my initiation rite. Mother could see no reason to permit *me* to make such a choice myself. I was in no position to argue. For reasons still obscure to me, she decided that I ought to prepare a spice cake, though spice cake is a pastry that was never served in our house. Perhaps

Introduction xv

it had been the first recipe Mother herself had ever prepared, or it may be that she thought it to be a not too demanding introduction to the limitless world of cookery to which I was so eagerly seeking admission, a universe of incredible mystery to me then.

When the selection was finally determined, Mother sent Mary and me, teacher and pupil, back to the kitchen for my initiation. Mary told me first to wash my hands. Then she ordered me to read the recipe through several times. I read it again and again, nearly bursting with excitement at the prospect of actually confecting something with my very own, very clean hands. When I declared myself thoroughly familiar with the directions provided in the cookbook, Mary —probably in an attempt to discourage what she considered a frivolous and transient interest—compelled me to read them yet again. I complied without complaint, and without losing a jot of my zeal. At last she grudgingly conceded that I had read and reread the formula sufficiently. Then I was allowed to scamper about the large kitchen gathering together all the ingredients and utensils necessary for the manufacture of spice cake. I dutifully arranged them neatly on the wood surface of the kitchen table.

It was abundantly evident from the very beginning of this exercise that Mary wasn't going to prove an enthusiastic teacher. She resented my presence in a domain she knew to be *hers*. But I chose to ignore her unhappiness because— ingenue though I certainly was—I recognized the kitchen to be *my* domain as well.

Once the preparatory flourishes had been accomplished, Mary showed me how to light the oven—undoubtedly because she feared that I might blow up the house. To her relief, I daresay, I managed this essential preliminary without difficulty. Only then was I permitted to begin the actual process of making spice cake.

I buttered the cake pans, without knowing why that was necessary (it keeps the contents from sticking). At Mary's stern command I sifted the flour four times, without explanation of the reason for this repetition that seemed to me quite superfluous. (Only much later on did I learn that sifted flour is lighter and of a much more even consistency than it is as it comes from its original container.)

The next step was to measure out the sugar and butter. Mary showed me how to tap the metal cup gently on the table to be certain that the amount of sugar was exact. She reluctantly demonstrated how to use a knife to level off the measurement of butter called for.

"Now," she said, "cream the sugar and the butter. The mixture ought to be white when you've got them blended enough." That *seemed* reasonable, but it wasn't. For in fact, when it was ready for use, this material wasn't a pure white at all; it was pale yellow. But no such doubt was in my mind at the time, because Mary added that I should combine the sugar and butter with my *hands*—a proposal utterly charming to a child of eight. (I don't think enough has been written about the wholly sensual, tactile pleasures of this sort of activity in the kitchen.)

Mary failed to explain to me why the process of creaming those two ingredients was made easier by using my bare little hands. Later, I realized that the warmth of the flesh softened the butter, thus rendering it more blendable with the sugar.

The third step was to separate the eggs. Mary showed me how to do this—but she never cautioned me to use two small bowls, one for the whites and one for the yolks. Only after the separation took place should I have placed the yolks in a single large bowl, the whites in another. Naturally, a novice made a couple of mistakes while breaking the eggs and in this fashion made unusable not only those with which I'd erred, but the ones I'd previously broken correctly.

Another problem arose when I began to beat the yolks. What exactly did the writer of the cookbook mean by instructing me to "beat the yolks until they are yellow"? After all, they were yellow already. I understood that these directions referred to a specific shade of yellow, but *what* shade? Mary promised to tell me when I had whipped the eggs to the appropriate color. I started to beat them, pausing frequently to ask whether the tone was right yet—as children ask when a journey is going to end. She might have done me the kindness to explain that the shade desired was a great deal paler than the one I'd imagined—that it resembled a lemon.

Once the yolks had been beaten until they were of a satisfactory tint, yet another question posed itself: How was I to stir them into the mixture of butter, sugar, flour, and milk? Mary said that I should pour and stir very gently, making sure that my blending action moved in only one direction. I did as I was told, but I'm now persuaded that this matter of stirring in a single direction is of no consequence to the result—an old cook's tale.

Then came the beating of the egg whites. I believed Mary when she assured me that they were stiff enough. But after nearly forty years of continuous cooking, I have, in my chapter on eggs, encountered difficulties in describing precisely *how* I know when beaten egg whites are adequately stiff. In that chapter I've done my best, but I confess that it is more a matter of instinct and experience—a bit of mystique.

Mary did show me how to fold the whites of the eggs into the batter, demonstrating the care required to avoid knocking the air out of this combination by needless or reckless stirring. This procedure, too, is described in the egg chapter.

Finally, I put the finished batter into the buttered pans and set the pans in the oven. The resulting spice cakes were good. Nevertheless, I've never again baked a spice cake, nor have I ever wanted to. Preparing them hadn't at all proved the dramatic experience I'd anticipated. I was not transfigured by it.

Learning How but Not Why

I think there are two reasons why this first effort at cooking turned out to be so great a disillusionment. The first is that I didn't understand why the various processes I followed worked—why they transformed the basic ingredients of flour, butter, eggs, milk, and other materials into a batter, and why the batter, when exposed to the heat of the oven, was subsequently transformed into a light, delicious cake. Like most novices, I didn't use my reasoning powers. They wouldn't have explained to me the chemistry of soda and leavening agents, or the leavening properties of eggs, but they would have told me one essential: that exposing the batter to a dry heat has the effect of heating and drying, and that baking is a process of heating and drying.

The second reason for my disappointment was that, as a matter of fact, I hadn't really wanted to bake a cake in the first place. I'd wanted to prepare an entire meal—from the hors d'oeuvres to *crêpes Suzette*. I'd wanted to do exactly what Mary did, to cook all the time, not just once in a while —which is all that I was allowed to do when I was a child.

I certainly can't say that my introductory experience in the kitchen was very informative, either. But since I had no place to go but up, I obviously learned something—the meaning of yellow, folding, stirring, and sifting. So it went with me for a long time. I grew increasingly able as a cook. I came to know *what* I was doing, but for the most part I still didn't know *why* it worked as it did. It still didn't occur to me to use my intelligence with respect to cooking. Many years would pass before I would appreciate the relevance of the intellect to cooking. Great cooks are invariably people of considerable intelligence. Until I came to this realization, I religiously followed recipe instructions, practicing what I now describe as "ritual cooking"—what I learned by observing more experienced cooks at work—but still failing to understand the underlying reasons why various procedures produced the results they did, why given ingredients may be combined in a variety of ways to compose delicious finished dishes.

Cooking Has a Grammar of Its Own

It was many years later that I made what now seems to me the perfectly obvious discovery that is the most important single element of cooking: Cooking has a grammar of its own, just as language does. Once you've mastered these "grammatical" elements, you can be wholly at ease in your kitchen—whether you are preparing a simple or a complicated dish. Understanding of the grammar of cooking dispels any apprehension you may feel and allows you to rejoice in the sheer pleasure that comes from "perfect" comprehension. You'll become a happy cooker.

All who know me well chortle at my electing to use the metaphor of grammar in this book. I am not renowned for my expertise in English grammar. But despite this trifling handicap, I *do* perceive the exactitude of the comparison—the combination of letters to form words, of words and punctuation marks to form sentences, of paragraphs to form chapters, of chapters to form a book.

The Recipe Is a Sort of Shorthand

To carry the analogy one step farther, let me add that recipes are a sort of shorthand rendition of this grammar I've referred to. A case in point: The recipe at hand advises you to take a piece of steak one-half inch in thickness and salt and pepper it. Heat a frying pan and put into it two tablespoons of butter and one of oil (the introduction of oil allows you to increase the temperature at which you can cook). Place the meat in the pan. Brown it on one side, then on the other. That is a rather elaborate description of a process indicated by a single word: "sauté."

Learning the Fundamentals

The demands on a competent professional chef are such that he would accomplish little if he were obliged to divide his attention between references to a cookbook and the actual cooking to be done. All of his time must be devoted to the cooking. In order to function on this very high level, he has to know by heart all the fundamentals—the complete grammar. He must, for instance, know how to make all the basic sauces on which are predicated countless subtle variations. With this profound awareness of the elements, he can afford to be inventive, innovative, creative. This is how he sustains his interest in the art of cooking, day after day. The aim of everyone who aspires to be more than a routine cook must be to attain a similar familiarity with these same elements of cooking style, with the result that when you use a recipe it is for quick reference only, to estimate measurements and quantities required, nothing more.

The purpose of this book is to enable you to grasp these elements of culinary grammar—the keys that help to make cooking easy and pleasant, that disclose to you the shorthand of recipes, that help you to think in cooking terms as you think in English terms, that eliminate any need to have a fear of failure. I also seek to make two basic points. The first is that while no two recipes are exactly alike, many of the processes employed are similar, often identical. To sauté is to sauté is to sauté. The second point is that the planning of a meal, like the composition of a perfect sentence, is a genuine art form. The grammatical metaphor is wholly applicable here as well. Like certain kinds of clauses which cannot be made to work harmoniously in combination, there are certain kinds of dishes which, though each is wonderful in itself, will not go together to make a harmonious meal.

Like linguistic grammar, the grammar of the kitchen offers virtually unlimited possibilities for variation. Sometimes you will simply prepare a steak sauté; sometimes you'll serve it with *sauce béarnaise*—thus going from utter simplicity to considerable complexity by the addition of an extremely subtle and savory sauce to the same primary ingredient: a piece of steak. These two good dishes are totally different culinary experiences.

I hope to offer a means by which you may acquire a thorough comprehension of these basic principles, the grammar of the kitchen and the shorthand of recipes. If the book achieves its purpose, you'll be able to read a recipe's terse instructions with perfect aplomb, or at least without fear! Armed with this understanding, you'll no longer feel the frequent need to make use of the prepared soups and sauces that make so much everyday cooking a bore when it ought to be as pleasant an experience as any other aspect of daily life which you *do* enjoy now. For in serving a fine meal, prepared calmly, you offer your family and guests an opportunity to share in something that you've done yourself—with pleasure.

As for the shorthand, let me illustrate the point by citing the recipe for spice cake which I consulted more than forty years ago:

> Sift flour; cream sugar and butter; stir yolks into mixture of flour, creamed sugar and butter, milk, and spices; beat whites until stiff; fold whites into mixture; bake batter in two greased pans in moderate oven until brown.

There are so many ellipses in that simple formula, points that its author regarded as matters of common knowledge. Frequently, however, the elements omitted are *not* common knowledge. That, essentially, is the purpose of this little book: to make plain what is not plain, to elucidate the elements of kitchen grammar and its recipe shorthand.

For every person who must spend time in the kitchen, cooking should be reinforced with the same sort of knowledge that is the secret of success of master chefs. If you acquire this understanding—which is not at all mind-bending in its complexity—then the aspect of drudgery which makes so many women and men unhappy or uncomfortable while doing culinary work can be completely and permanently eliminated. It will make you feel free to improve, to have fun, to be a happy cooker. Since we all *have* to cook, why not do it both well and happily?

It is my hope that this will be as useful a volume to you as Fowler or Strunk or *A Manual of Style* are to writers—an instant resource in moments of crisis. I hope, too, that my annotated and highly opinionated bibliography will lead you to cookbooks that have given me (and those who have eaten at my table) such great pleasure.

The Grammar of Cooking systematically investigates and explains the fundamental skills and principles essential to every cook who really cares about the quality of the dishes she or he serves, and about the propriety of putting them together to comprise ideal menus.

The Grammar of Cooking

1

A Simple Subject: *Roasting, Broiling, Panbroiling, Spit-Roasting*

Philadelphia Dinners

In the epoch and the society in which I was brought up, the traveler, on returning home from Europe, dispensed with the succulent and fattening foods which she or he had enjoyed while abroad. Great eating was associated almost exclusively with the total experience of holiday, something special and distinct from everyday life. My parents shared this feeling.

There *were* some exceptions to this rule, however. Perhaps for a special dinner party an exotic dish would be produced, but this was a rarity, for it occasioned a case of nervous exhaustion in the kitchen—not because the dish itself was so difficult or so time-consuming to prepare, but because it was alien to a staff which was governed by a routine of what we still refer to as "good plain cooking." Plain it certainly was, and good as well, for the finest ingredients were always employed. It was the very best quality of "plain cooking."

Our Sunday dinner always featured a "joint," as the English describe a substantial roast. Stew was a favorite dish, too, but it was intended only for family consumption, for Mother considered it a little too "common" to be served to guests. Steaks were for special occasions—like the eve of a child's departure for boarding school or the dinner following her return from that kind of exclusive captivity.

The menus of good, planly cooked fare would be varied, of course, but were principally dependent on the changing of the seasons. We had shad and shad roe in the early spring, and sweet corn in August. A beef roast consisting of the first three or four ribs (the best of that cut) was winter fare, to be replaced in summer by fried chicken. Since we lived near Philadelphia, of which my paternal ancestors had long been natives, there were some particular local dishes to be presented: creamed kidneys for summer breakfasts, scrapple in winter, and Philadelphia fried tomatoes when tomatoes were readily available. Terrapin Maryland would be ordered out from Holland's, a celebrated Philadelphia catering firm, for especially gala dinners. Another local delicacy prepared outside our own kitchen was pistachio ice cream combined with crushed frozen strawberries, served in a melon-shaped mold. This was shipped out from Salter's on the Main Line commuter train in the care of the baggage master. It was transported in a uniquely designed leather tub which was filled with ice and rock salt and covered with burlap.

In this way, with a number of variations, the seasons succeeded each other, year after year, before the onset of World War II. Afterward, these delicacies vanished—as did the baggage master from the Paoli local. Salter's closed its doors. Terrapin Maryland is bloody expensive and nigh on impossible to prepare satisfactorily at home. However, if you have a freezer, you can easily make pistachio ice cream and crushed strawberries.

Discovering June Platt

A couple of years before that war started in Europe, my mother came home with a new cookbook. This one, however, did not reside on the kitchen shelf reserved for such staple reference works as Fanny Farmer and Mrs. Moody and other standbys. Instead, it remained in a bookcase in her bedroom, to be consulted only when guests were expected for dinner. It was in this fashion that I first became acquainted with June Platt's *Party Cook Book* (inexplicably unavailable today). That volume was my very first *literary* and literate introduction to great cooking. What an initiation to the fine literature of the kitchen! What a reawakening of the taste buds first stirred in Europe during my early childhood! With the passage of the years, a few other books have joined June Platt on my personal list of culinary masterpieces for which my respect is nearly absolute. But she, like those meals abroad when I was only six, was a sort of revelation and is still a beacon by which I'm guided.

Good Red Meat

Most of us like roasts and chops and steaks. When the meats are good and well prepared, they are delicious, and they are endowed with a quality which we tend to think of as completely American—a chauvinistic attitude that *foreign* cooks share about these very same cuts. We're not unique at all. It is these kinds of cuts of meat that I want to discuss initially. Since they represent by far the most expensive portions, and since these are the ones you roast or broil or spit-roast or panbroil, you should understand the techniques involved in choosing as well as preparing them for the table. We are better able to reconcile ourselves to the expenditure of appalling sums when we feel we have done justice to them when we present them for the consumption of family and friends.

First Cuts

Why *are* these cuts of meat so terribly dear (inflationary questions quite apart)? The answer is twofold: They are in great demand, and—in proportion to the size of any carcass—there are fewer first cuts than others. That's why these sections are described as "first cuts." For most of us, they are a first choice because of their qualities of tenderness and flavor.

Since meat is muscle, the muscles which are found in first cuts are the most tender—the least developed. The muscular tissue that contains the greatest amount of fat "marbling" is the best, and there is also considerable fat surrounding these portions. The renowned tenderness of the beef filet, though less marbled than steak, derives from the fact that it is a muscle which is little used by the steer. In spite of its enormous price, filet may often prove a very good buy because it is so rich that the average diner eats much less of it than of other first cuts. It is much more filling, for example, than steak. The first cuts have one other significant feature in common: They are the juiciest. It is this combination of fattiness and juiciness that makes it possible for first cuts to withstand the rigors of roasting, broiling, panbroiling, and spit-roasting. With the exception of very thick hamburger (which normally has a high amount of fat in it), other cuts require the addition of liquid to make them tender after cooking.

The observations made about beef apply equally to veal, lamb, and pork. The prices of certain cuts will differ slightly; a rib lamb chop, for instance, is the most expensive of lamb cuts. The thin slices of veal known to the Italians as *scaloppini*, though they come from the calf's leg, are the dearest of veal cuts because of the high demand, and their special bias cutting which causes waste.

Get to Know Your Butcher

Where should such fine first cuts of meat be purchased? If you happen to be lucky enough to have a friend or a friendly relation who is a butcher, you must cherish him, coddle him, spoil him, bribe and corrupt him. Do anything you must in order to remain in his favor and to induce him always to think of you first. If you don't have a sympathetic relationship with your butcher, you're simply not going to secure the best cuts of meat in his supply.

The laying out of large quantities of cash is no guarantee that when your butcher enters the seclusion of his cold-storage room, his eye will come to rest on the finest side of meat to bring out for your inspection. If you haven't yet established a cordial acquaintance with a butcher, my advice is to shop around the area in which you live in the hope of finding an old-fashioned butcher, one who knows and loves his craft. It's not merely a matter of his skill in cutting a piece of meat. If his supplies haven't been well selected and properly and sufficiently hung, they may be tender but they'll lack the most delicate flavor obtainable, though they be of the best prime or choice selections. Proper hanging is required; that is a major part of the secret of flavorful meat—first cut or not.

If you live in or near a neighborhood where the European traditions are still very much alive, you may be fortunate, for the chances are good that an important segment of that population is accustomed to spending a far greater proportion of income on food than is the case for most "Americans." European standards demand a quality of meat and produce that the rest of us have been compelled, by prepackaging and mass merchandising, to think impossible of attainment any longer. Shopping in such a neighborhood may be a little like traveling abroad, and it will certainly be all the more enjoyable if your concern is for first-rate ingredients. If you show a genuine interest and a desire to learn, I promise you'll find an enthusiastic response which often is of far more avail than the swaggering flourish of a fat purse.

But wherever and however you find a butcher of skill with a supply of high quality, make him your dear friend. My butcher is of Lebanese extraction. He and I have enjoyed a long and wholly sympathetic friendship. I admire Edmund Dimyan's choices of meats, and he respects my enthusiasm. He's always pleased when, after he's sold me an exceptionally fine cut, I express my gratitude. He invariably cuts the meat as I ask him to, because he appreciates how important this is to the outcome of the dish I'm planning to serve.

Only once in my life have I succeeded in making anything like a satisfactory acquaintance with a butcher in a supermarket. This occurred during a comparatively brief stay in Cooperstown, New York. Otherwise, I've been disappointed and disillusioned by all my supermarket experiences where high quality was an issue. Those mirrored panels that conceal the butchering operations, and those bells to sound for "personal service" produce bored, uninterested meat packagers who defeat me utterly, make me feel that I'm dealing not with talented artisans who are justifiably proud of their skills, but with automatons who are managed by a vast, remote computer that's out of my control—and out of theirs as well. Nevertheless, I *do* check out supermarkets when I'm seeking cheaper cuts of meat—though frequently the fancy butcher's prices are competitive. There are some dishes where marinating or long cooking times would make it blasphemous to use cuts of top quality. It's not merely inappropriate; tenderer cuts simply disintegrate in that sort of cooking process. As in selecting just the right word for a phrase, *it is essential to select the right piece of meat for the dish you're planning to make.*

Standard Cuts of Meat

Since this book went to press the United States Government standardized labeling for retail cuts of beef. All cuts

Roasting, Broiling, Panbroiling, Spit-Roasting

of beef when sold to the public must be properly labeled. The following listing may be obtained in chart form, showing precisely how each cut should look, from the National Live Stock and Meat Board:

BRISKET
  Fresh Brisket
  Corned Brisket

CHUCK
  Boneless Chuck Eye Roast
  Blade Roast or Steak
  Boneless Shoulder Pot
    Roast or Steak
  Beef for Stew
  Chuck Short Ribs
  Arm Pot Roast or Steak
  Cross Rib Pot Roast
  Ground Beef

FLANK
  Ground Beef
  Beef Patties
  Flank Steak
  Flank Steak Rolls

FORE SHANK
  Shank Cross Cuts
  Beef for Stew

RIB
  Rib Roast
  Rib Steak
  Rib Steak, Boneless
  Rib Eye (Delmonico)
    Roast or Steak

ROUND
  Round Steak
  Top Round Steak
  Bottom Round Roast
    or Steak
  Eye of Round
  Heel of Round
  Roiled Rump
  Cubed Steak
  Ground Beef

SHORT LOIN
  Top Loin Steak
  T-Bone Steak
  Porterhouse Steak
  Boneless Top Loin Steak
  Tenderloin (Filet Mignon)
    Steak or Roast

SHORT PLATE
  Short Ribs
  Beef for Stew
  Skirt Steak Rolls
  Ground Beef

SIRLOIN
  Pin Bone Sirloin Steak
  Flat Bone Sirloin Steak
  Wedge Bone Sirloin Steak
  Boneless Sirloin Steak

TIP
  Tip Steak
  Tip Roast
  Tip Kabobs

The Grading of Meats

All meats and poultry are inspected by representatives of the United States Department of Agriculture. All are graded according to quality—except for pork. Why pork should be an exception, I haven't been able to discover. The grade appears on the label attached to poultry. It's stamped over and over again on meat carcasses. The law requires that each cut bear at least a portion of this grading stamp at the time you purchase it. However, don't be surprised if you're unable to find it.

Here is a list of the grades of meat normally available in butcher shops and supermarkets:

PRIME: Beef, lamb, veal
CHOICE: Beef, lamb, veal
GOOD: Beef, lamb, veal

A butcher purchases pork from a wholesaler according to an informal (i.e., nongovernmental) rating of "A, B, C, or D," the grading determined by the quantity of fat on the carcass. Grade "A," the fattest, is thought the best. Very lean American pork will never be tender, no matter how long it is marinated.

There *are* lower grades of government-inspected meat. These, however, are primarily for the use of institutions that don't have to concern themselves unduly about pleasing those whom they serve. I've never seen these cuts offered in a store for the consumption of the general public. If they *are* available, butchers understandably make no boast of the fact.

Physical Appearance of Meat

About the physical appearance of meat, I want to stress that no matter what its shade or color, *all* meat and domestic fowl must have a good, *clear* look. It's a little difficult to define this clarity of appearance in words. Even if the shade of a piece of meat or a fowl seems right to you, avoid it if it seems lackluster. When you next have a look at some meat, perhaps you'll notice what I mean. The only luster is that afforded by the packaging.

The point in this respect about prepackaged meat is obvious: Nothing of importance is revealed beneath the plastic wrapping except color and weight. You can't determine whether the piece has been evenly sliced or what its tone and texture are. A product so displayed is no more recognizable than your own features would be if they were similarly enclosed. Moreover, it has been established that the bacteria count of the prepackaged product rises much more rapidly than one which is not so wrapped.

Following are some notes about appearances:

BEEF
The fat that surrounds a piece of beef should be waxy, with thin lines of white fat running through the flesh. This is "marbling." The color should be a good, bright red, pale or deep. When raw beef is sliced, its tone should be dark, clear purple. It only turns to the colors we associate with uncooked beef after some exposure to the air. (As noted earlier, filets of beef are *not* as marbled.)

LAMB
The carcass of a lamb should be compact. The leg should be plump—the plumper the better. The meat must be of a rose shade, not like the red of beef. Avoid lamb that is dark red or brownish in color.

VEAL
If a leg or chop of veal seems rather large to you, it is probably not proper veal. It's too old. The color should be pale pink. If it is red or brown, it has been around too long and thus can be used only for grinding or making soups. Veal usually has very little fat, and what there is of fat

should be white and glistening. You have to see *poor* veal in order to distinguish it readily from *good* veal. Since fine veal is difficult to find, you are most likely to locate it in an Italian neighborhood.

PORK
The meat of pork is of about the same shade of pink as veal. Avoid all pork whose color is very dark brown. Pork fat is noticeably whiter and greasier than that of beef or veal.

CHICKEN
A chicken whose skin is very white will have little flavor. The tone should be yellowish and fresh in appearance. The breastbone must be flexible, except that of an old bird which you plan to use only for boiling or fricassee.

TURKEY
The meat of turkey is white, with a bluish or pinkish undertone. Avoid a bruised turkey or one that has brown spots. The breastbone should be supple. My own preference is for "local" birds, which are increasingly harder to find. Again, a good independent butcher is the likeliest source.

OTHER FOWL
Ducks, geese, pheasants, squabs, game hens, etc., are almost impossible to purchase except frozen and in plastic wrapping that makes serious examination of condition out of the question. You just have to take it on faith that they will prove tasty and tender. Your best assurance is to buy them from a merchant you trust or, especially in the instances of duck and game hen, to purchase brands you have tried and found satisfactory.

FISH
The eye of a fresh fish is clear, the skin slippery to the touch, the meat firm and springy, the interior of the gills a reddish

brown and clean. Don't buy a fish that has been already scaled. The scales should be difficult to pull out. Its odor should be not too remarkably fishy. Do *not* keep uncooked fish for more than twenty-four hours, and wrap it carefully and completely in odor-proof material before placing it in your refrigerator, for otherwise the smell will soon permeate everything else in storage there, even if you keep an opened carton of bicarbonate of soda there—a very good idea, for it is a fine deodorant. If you plan to serve fish cold, cook it ahead and cover it well. You ought to allow ½ pound of fish per serving, though ⅓ pound will suffice for fillets and steaks. These weights should be calculated *after* the head and tail have been removed. A well-cooked fish is *great* food, and fish leftovers help to make excellent salads and creamed dishes. There are many wonderful seafood preparations that deserve further investigation—soups and stews, for example, and baked fish. It's not necessary always to buy fish steaks or fillets.

The Right Size for the Purpose
A major point in the purchase of meat is consideration of the size of the piece you require for the task you propose. This, of course, is determined mainly by the number of people you plan to serve and the other items on the menu you've devised. In terms of weight, the most you'll need per individual serving is 8 ounces. But you should also take into account whether or not you want some leftovers to serve cold or to make into hash or some other cooked dish. *The size of the cut should determine your choice of meat or poultry or fish.*

ROASTING

It would be silly and unreasonable to suggest that roasting is an easy way to cook. It requires time and experience to master. There are, however, some things you can do to help avoid failure. As I've already pointed out, the choice of cut can be vital, and you should know the exact weight of the piece after it has been trimmed and barded.

Roasting is a dry heat procedure. The meat is placed on a trivet or rack in the roasting pan so that the heat of the oven envelops the cut as completely as possible. A trivet is not required for a standing rib roast, since it is raised by the bones above the bottom of the pan.

There are many factors to take into account when you are roasting: the length of time the meat has hung, its age, the diameter of the cut. In roasting, the heat travels from the outside inward toward the center; a 4-pound and an 8-pound roast of the same diameter will cook in the same amount of time. The only way to be sure about cooking times is to use a roasting thermometer; the degree of cooking is determined by the temperature achieved at the center of the cut, something you can only know from a thermometric reading.

Old cooking hands can decide when a piece of meat has been cooked sufficiently merely by touching it. They push it with a finger. The spongier it is, the greater the measure of doneness. You can learn this by making use of a thermometer and simultaneously palpating the piece at various stages, thus acquiring the necessary expertise. A time chart is furnished to give you a rough idea of the periods required for cooking various cuts of meat to various degrees of doneness (see pp. 21–23).

Veal, pork, and all fowl except game birds should be thoroughly cooked—well done. These you can test by pricking the surface and observing the color of the juices that flow out. In all instances the fluid should be clear, without a tinge of pink. The juices of lamb, a meat which few like to eat rare, should be pale pink. Again, the thermometer will offer an accurate guide. The final steps of roasting are the most critical; a few added minutes can mean an overcooked piece of meat.

Since the juices of your roast are boiling as they travel

from the exterior to the interior of the cut, it means that for ten or twenty minutes after you have stopped applying heat, depending on the diameter of the piece, the cooking process continues. This must be taken into account in your calculation of time requirements for roasting.

The thermometer should be inserted in such a way that its tip is located at the very center of the cut to be roasted. It must not, however, be allowed to come to rest against a piece of bone, for the bone will always be hotter than the meat surrounding it.

No liquid should ever be introduced into the roasting process, nor should the meat ever be allowed to sit in melted fat. If you add liquids such as water, wine, or stock, your meat will be steamed, not roasted.

About Plastics and Foils in Roasting

I want to make an observation about the so-called "roasting bags" made of plastic and the use of aluminum foil for roasting. In neither application does one actually *roast* at all. The very act of wrapping a piece of meat or a fowl makes it, by definition, a steaming process. Both methods, though they do spare you a little labor and help to keep your oven clean, are to be avoided because they give a completely different flavor to the dish than the proper roasting method does. You may like the effect their employment has on lamb and pork, but the bald fact is that steaming alters the texture as well as the taste of the dish and separates the fibers, tending to make the flesh soggy instead of merely properly moist.

Cuts of Meat for Roasting

BEEF
  Rolled rump
  Standing rump
  Standing rib roast (the first three ribs are the best)
  Rolled rib roast
  Silver tip
  Sirloin eye round
  Filet

LAMB
  Leg
  Boneless leg
  Crown roast
  Rolled shoulder roast
  Rolled loin
  Rolled breast (which is fatty)
  Rack of lamb

VEAL
  Standing rump roast
  Rolled rump roast
  Crown roast
  Rib roast
  Blade roast
  Arm roast
  Rolled shoulder roast
  Leg center cut
  Round roast
  Breast

PORK
  Loin roast
  Boneless loin roast
  Tenderloin
  Crown roast
  Boston butt
  Smoked shoulder
  Cushion picnic shoulder
  Fresh rolled shoulder
  Fresh ham
  Fresh picnic shoulder
  Spareribs
  Rolled fresh ham
  Ham (variously preserved)

CHICKENS (IN ORDER OF SIZE AND AGE)
  Broilers
  Fryers
  Roasters
  Stewers (also used for stews and fricassees)
  Capons (The ultimate in chicken is an emasculated rooster, unsurpassed for roasting and usually well worth the higher price you must pay for it, since the ratio of meat to bone is much greater than for chickens. The capon's meat, which is more delicate than chicken's in flavor, adds to its deserved reputation for quality.)

TURKEYS

The range in size of turkeys today runs from ones of less than 10 pounds to the great Thanksgiving and Christmas monsters of 20 pounds or more. Turkeys are almost always roasted, although, as noted below, the smaller ones may also be broiled. (They are suitable for boiling, too.)

DUCKS AND GEESE, GUINEA HENS, SQUABS, AND GAME HENS

These are primarily for roasting also, but may be cooked as well *en casserole*. All fowl, with the exception of ducks and geese, should be barded with fatback of pork or salt pork for roasting purposes, or smeared with butter.

A Note About Barding: Sometimes confused with "larding," barding consists of wrapping the roast or fowl with a piece of fat or suet. This should be done to any roast which is not endowed with a substantial coating of fat of its own. Pork, lamb, goose, and duck are well supplied with natural fat and normally don't require barding. The procedure involves fatback of pork or salt pork for fowl or veal, and good suet for beef. The open surface of the meat should first be rubbed with good beef drippings or bacon fat; the fowl with butter or bacon fat—*never* with margarine, which burns, i.e., separates into particles which begin to char at too low a temperature.

Since pork and fowl are not graded so meticulously as other meat products by the Department of Agriculture, you'll occasionally find good poultry and pork in your supermarket. When I'm planning to serve pork and certain poultry dishes, I always check there first to see if the supply on hand is of suitable quality. After all, why should you pay more than you need to?

Maxims for Selecting and Roasting Meats

Not long ago, I watched a woman purchase a pot roast of beef that weighed only a pound and a half. How could a piece of meat only an inch and a half thick survive two or three hours of cooking? The question is rhetorical. It couldn't survive long enough to gain its flavor without decomposing almost completely.

- Never try to prepare a standing rib roast of less than three ribs. No matter how sharp your carving knife, you'll find the slicing of the last inch more often impossible than merely difficult.

- Never roast *any* piece of meat which, because of its size, requires *less* than one hour's cooking time, because less than 60 minutes is inadequate for the roasting process. If you prefer red meat, you should allow 15 minutes per pound. In other words, a roast to be served rare should *never* weigh less than 4 pounds. This rule holds equally for a pot roast (discussed in Chapter 6).

- The shape of the roast is another important aspect in making your choice of cut. A piece like a silver tip or an eye round, with a small diameter, is best for a little roast. Because of their compact shape, boned roasts are good value. You have better control of the roasting process. For one thing, the bone serves to give the piece needless bulk. Because of the convection of the heat by the bone, a roast which retains it will cook more rapidly than one from which it has been removed.

- In the case of roasts, it is the *diameter*, not the length or weight, that determines cooking time. A roast that is 3 inches thick will require an hour to cook and a resting period of 10 minutes (I'll explain about "resting" later on). A roast that is 6 inches in diameter needs 2¼ hours in the oven.

Your Oven

A vital aspect of successful roasting *and* baking and any other cooking that occurs in the oven is to be completely familiar with the characteristics of your own stove. It may be worthwhile to purchase an oven thermometer in order to be sure that the temperature control of your oven is relatively accurate. If it isn't, you should try to have it adjusted. If this can't be managed, then you'll just have to experiment until you're certain of your oven's idiosyncrasies, as one becomes familiar with the peculiarities of an aging car.

Techniques of Roasting

For roasting, the shelf of your oven should be as close to the top as you can arrange it, given the size of the cut and utensil employed. This is because the heat rises. The closer the roast is to the top of the oven, the greater the amount of dry heat it will be subjected to. If your stove is electric and its heating element is set in the top of the oven, you should be guided by the instruction book that came with the appliance.

Place all meat (including a standing rib roast) *top* side up.

All meat should be at room temperature before you begin to cook it.

BASTING

Basting consists of bathing the roast in its own juices. It is one of the most voluptuous and most satisfying of all the elements of cooking—opening the oven door, feeling the heat, smelling the aroma of the roast, drawing the drippings into a syringe or scooping them into a basting spoon and releasing them all over the cooking meat. It is a pure sensual delight. You should baste your roast every 15 or 20 minutes. Take up the juices in a syringe, a spoon, or—for poultry—a feather brush, and cover every exposed surface.

I add salt and pepper *after* the first basting has been completed. Otherwise they simply run off, leaving the meat unseasoned and making the juices in the bottom of the pan excessively salty.

Roasting Temperatures

There are two popular and about equally accepted theories regarding the temperatures to employ for roasting. The newer one calls for a low, constant heat. The meat, begun at room temperature, is placed in a *preheated* oven of 300°–

350° (allow at least 20 minutes for the oven to attain maximum temperature). In low-heat roasting, you may turn the heat up to 450°–500° for the final 20 minutes in order to give the piece a satisfactorily brown shade. The argument for low, constant heat is that it makes for more juice and less shrinkage of the cut.

But I think there is a significant difference of flavor from that obtained by the older high-heat method, which calls for the placing of the cut in a preheated oven of 450°–500° (which sears the meat at once). Searing closes the fibers of the surface by scorching them dry. The piece should be left at this temperature for the first 20 minutes of roasting. When you reduce the temperature to 350°, you should baste your roast for the first time. My personal preference is for this method.

Notes on Roasting Times

When you're calculating oven times for roasting, it is essential to remember the dimensions as well as the weight of the cut to be cooked.

Another factor to be kept in mind is that all meat or fowl coming from the oven should be allowed to "rest" for at least 20 minutes before being brought to the table—a period which permits the juices literally to stop dancing around. Because of the tendency of the roast to retain the heat of the oven, it will continue to cook for at least 10 minutes after emerging. This element should be included in your estimate of cooking times. In fact, if you have made use of the newer method, with the heat turned up very high at the end of the roasting process, you ought to allow the dish a rest period of 25 minutes before presenting it. Resting also makes carving easier.

It is important to remember that the following tables are rules of thumb, and the times that I recommend are not to be taken as absolutes. Less cooking time is required for pieces containing large quantities of fat or pieces of small diameter. It must be understood that at the time they are introduced to the oven, all pieces to be roasted are at room temperature.

TABLE I. TIME TABLES FOR ROASTING
All the timings include periods of searing and resting.

BEEF

		HIGH-HEAT METHOD (Sear meat 20–30 minutes at 500°, then reduce temperature to 350°.)	LOW-HEAT METHOD (Preheated oven is at 325°; turn to 500° for final 20 minutes.)
Degree of cooking	Thermometer reading	Minutes per pound	Minutes per pound
Rare	110°–115° (bone in)	18	20
Med. rare	120°–125° (bone out)	32	34
Medium	125°–130° (bone in)	22	25
	(bone out)	38	40
Well done	145°–150° (bone in)	27	30
	(bone out)	48	50

LAMB

				HIGH-HEAT METHOD (Sear meat for 20 minutes at 450°; reduce temperature to 350°.)	LOW-HEAT METHOD (Oven is at 300°–325°.)
Cut	Degree of cooking	Thermometer reading		Minutes per pound	Minutes per pound
Leg and loin	Medium	175°	(bone in)	10–12	25–30
			(bone out)	25–30	35–40
	Well done	180°	(bone in)	13–15	30–35
			(bone out)	30–35	40–45
Crown roast	Medium	175°		10	15
	Well done	180°		15	20
Shoulder	Medium	175°	(bone in)	30	35–40
	Well done	180°	(bone out)	40	45
Rolled breast		175°–180°		40	45

NOTE: *Resting time for lamb is 15 minutes.*

VEAL

(Sauté to brown a veal roast before cooking in oven. Cook veal at a constant temperature of 325° and always serve it well done, at a thermometer reading of 160°.)

Cut	Minutes per pound
Leg and rump	25–30
Sirloin, loin, standing rib	40–45
Shoulder	25
Stuffed shoulder or breast	40–45

PORK

(All pork should be cooked to a thermometer temperature of 165°–170°. It should be browned by sautéing and cooked at a constant temperature of 350°.)

Cut	Minutes per pound
Leg	30–45
Tenderloin	35
Sirloin Boston butt	45–50
Boneless sirloin	50
Loin and groin	35–40
Shoulder (bone in)	30–35
Boned shoulder	40–45
Cushion	35–40
Spareribs	35

CURED PORK

Cut	Thermometer reading	Minutes per pound	Oven temperature
Uncooked ham (mild cure)			
large	165°	15–18	300°
medium	165°	18–22	300°
small	165°	22–25	300°
Precooked ham (mild cure)	130°	15–20	325°

Cut	Thermometer reading	Minutes per pound	Oven temperature
Country-cured ham (after simmering)	130°	45–60	350°
Canadian bacon (whole piece)	160°	25	350°
Smoked shoulder butt	170°	40	300°
Smoked picnic shoulder	170°	35	300°

FILET
(No searing)

Degree of cooking	Thermometer reading	Minutes per pound	Oven temperature
Rare	140°	40–60 depending on diameter	450°
Medium	160°		

TECHNIQUES OF ROASTING FOWL

After many years of cooking, I have come to agree with Mapie, the Countess de Toulouse-Lautrec, that the best roast chicken is cooked at a constant high temperature (450°–500°) for something like an hour—depending on the peculiarities of your oven. The skin may not be the crispest obtainable, but what is more important is the flavor, moisture, and tenderness of the bird itself; and this method assures these superiorities. In China, where crisp duck skin is a delicacy greatly valued, the creature is roasted solely for the purpose of obtaining this feature. The meat of the duck is not served at table. The fact is that it is virtually impossible to have a fowl perfectly cooked inside with a crisp skin —except if you spit-roast it.

Regardless of the heat technique you follow, to assure yourself a juicy chicken or turkey you should place the fowl breast side *down* on the trivet. It is remarkable how much juicier the result; for the fat beneath the fowl's skin, especially that along its back, melts downward into the breast when it is roasted in this fashion. The quality of the thighs and legs is also improved thus by their greater exposure to the heat.

For the final 20 minutes of roasting (final 30–40 minutes for a large turkey), turn the bird over. If you have been using low heat, turn the oven temperature up by 100° in order somewhat to brown and crisp the skin.

You must be extremely careful not to puncture the surface of your meat or fowl during the roasting and basting process. This is especially difficult to avoid when you're turning over a bird. There are gadgets available to facilitate this operation. My own, for large turkeys and big pieces of meat, is rather primitive—I use a large bath towel.

With the exception of ducks and geese, all should be barded. As with meats, the wisest way to determine when they are cooked is to use a thermometer.

I roast *small* game birds, Cornish hens, and squabs in a 450° oven for 45 minutes, then turn them over, breast up, for the final 15 minutes, roasting them an hour in all and giving them a resting period of 10 minutes.

A *stuffed* small bird requires 15–20 minutes longer in the oven. The test to determine whether a bird is thoroughly cooked is to prick the second joint or thigh; if the juice runs clear, it is done.

Capons, roasting chickens, and turkeys are begun in a very hot oven (450°–500°) for 20 minutes, then the heat is reduced to 350° for the balance of the roasting time, which is 20 minutes per pound (including the weight of the stuffing, if any). I turn them breast up for the final 30 minutes, so that they are a lovely brown all over. The rest period is 20 minutes, except for a turkey of more than 20 pounds, which rests only 15 minutes or so. If you are able to find a fresh turkey and willing to pay the much greater price, temperature rules are nearly useless, for these birds roast much more rapidly than do frozen ones—anywhere from 60 to 90 minutes more quickly.

My own preference is to braise geese and ducks rather than to roast them. However, if I *do* roast them, I first sear them on top of the stove after pricking their breasts. The purpose of this operation is to draw off excess fat. Afterward, they are placed into a 350° oven and roasted at the rate of 20 minutes per pound of oven-ready weight, stuffed or not.

Birds such as pheasant and guinea hen may be roasted in the manner of chickens. However, as with geese and ducks, I prefer to braise them.

In the case of *wild* duck, follow the recipe of a good cookbook. I don't like wild duck and never serve it anymore.

Saving Grease from Fowl: The grease from cooking fowl of all sorts should be saved; it is unbeatable for use in preparing other dishes such as the sautéing of vegetables and sweetbreads.

Making Stock from Fowl: Even when roasting, you may want to pour white wine over the fowl for the final 15-minute period of cooking, after you've basted it for the last time. While the roasting is going on I place wing tips, neck, giblets, and aromatic vegetables in a saucepan with water so as to make a cup or more of stock. Then I mix at the end with the juices left in the bottom of the roasting pan. (See Chapter 9.) I store the liver in my liver bank in the freezer until I've accumulated enough for whatever purpose I have in mind for them.

TECHNIQUES OF ROASTING FISH

I love roast fish. As a rule I stuff them, then roast them on a *mirepoix* or *matignon* (see pp. 76, 77). I use a high-heat technique—anywhere from 40 to 60 minutes, depending on the size. When it is done, the fish will be flaky (you can feel it give way when you press it). In the case of salmon, I don't use a dry-heat process, but wrap the fish (after buttering it well, adding salt and pepper) in aluminum foil and roast it for an hour in the case of a large fish; a smaller fish will take less cooking time.

BROILING

Broiling is another method of dry-heat cooking, where the flame plays directly on the meat. It is to be used for small and/or flat cuts of meat, thin as well as thick.

Like ovens, broiler thermostats differ significantly from stove to stove.

Not to be overlooked are the excellent and convenient small electric broiling units. It's wise in all instances to follow the directions provided by the manufacturer of the appliance.

Cuts of Meat for Broiling

BEEF
- Ground beef patties (hamburgers, too, provided they are at least ½ inch thick)
- Sirloin steaks
- Pinbone steaks
- Porterhouse steaks
- T-bone steaks
- Club steaks
- Rib steaks
- Contrefilets
- Filets

LAMB
- Patties
- Leg steaks
- Rib chops
- Saratoga chops
- Boneless shoulder chops
- Loin chops
- English chops

VEAL

Veal should *not* be broiled. There isn't enough juice in the meat to allow for broiling. Consequently, broiling serves to dry it out intolerably. The smaller cuts of veal should be panfried or sautéed, for which see p. 43.

PORK
 Canadian bacon
 Loin chops
 Sliced shoulder butt
 Ham slices
 Bacon

FOWL
 Broiling chickens
 Capons
 Rock Cornish hens
 Squabs

Note: All fowl for broiling should be split in half down the back, with the wing joint broken so that it may be spread out flat. (Remove the spine and save for use in stock.) The inside should be broiled first, then the outside. Butter the inside and add salt and pepper before you begin, repeating the process when you reverse it.

SEAFOOD
 Fillets of fish
 Fish steaks (notably salmon, haddock, swordfish, etc.)
 Lobsters and other crustaceans

Techniques of Broiling

Whenever you broil a piece of meat that has an edge of fat, the edge should be scored. Make a series of sharp, shallow cuts in the fat to prevent it from causing the meat to curl as the fat melts and crispens.

My own methods of broiling depend entirely on the object to be prepared. For a good thick piece of beef or lamb, I set the broiler temperature at its maximum setting and place the shelf at its highest possible location, taking into account the thickness of the cut. This is for the purpose of searing the meat. I first allow the broiling pan and its rack to become extremely hot. I rub the rack with some suet from the meat, working as quickly as possible so as not to allow it to cool any more than is absolutely necessary.

After coating the meat with softened sweet butter, I put it on the rack, which (as I've noted) I place as close as may be to the source of heat. After one side has been seared, I reverse it, using two spatulas in order not to puncture the surface already sealed. Following the time chart that is applicable, I reverse it one more time. If the cut is exceptionally thick, I reduce the temperature or move the broiler pan to a lower position in order to prevent excessive scorching of the surface.

In the cases of the "white" meats, like pork and chicken and thin cuts of lamb or beef, I don't place them so close to the heat in the first instance, since they require longer but slower cooking than do thicker cuts of lamb or beef. If one used the same broiler position and the same high heats, these pieces of chicken and pork would char too much on the outside, while the inside would be raw and inedible. Thin slices of lamb and beef would emerge from the broiler with the appearance and texture of burned toast.

If, while being broiled, the meat you are cooking seems to be drying out, apply butter or an oily marinade (or a barbecue sauce, which is really more or less the same thing) to add the necessary moisture.

Warning: Under no circumstances should broiled meats be basted in their own pan juices, since the juices at the bottom of your broiling pan get very hot and take on a burned and unpleasant taste.

TABLE II. TIME TABLES FOR BROILING STEAKS

(High position in broiler, medium flame: 350°)

Sirloin

Thickness	Minutes Rare	Medium
1 inch	10, 1st side	12, 1st side
	6, 2nd side	8, 2nd side
1½ inch	20, 1st side	17, 1st side
	15, 2nd side	11, 2nd side
2 inch	20, 1st side	22, 1st side
	17, 2nd side	19, 2nd side

Note: If the cut is more than 2 inches in thickness, sear both sides first, then broil it about 20 minutes per side. Make a small incision to determine whether it needs more cooking or not.

Porterhouse

Thickness	Minutes Rare	Medium
1 inch	10, 1st side	12, 1st side
	5, 2nd side	7, 2nd side
1½ inch	15, 1st side	17, 1st side
	9, 2nd side	11, 2nd side
2 inch	20, 1st side	22, 1st side
	14, 2nd side	18, 2nd side

Club Steak

Thickness	Minutes Rare	Medium
1 inch	7, 1st side	10, 1st side
	5, 2nd side	7, 2nd side
1½ inch	12, 1st side	15, 1st side
	9, 2nd side	11, 2nd side
2 inch	17, 1st side	22, 1st side
	14, 2nd side	18, 2nd side

FILET MIGNON
(Very high heat only)

| | Minutes per side | |
Thickness	Rare	Medium
1 inch	2–3	3–4
1½ inch	4–5	5–6
2 inch	5–6	7–8

LAMB CHOPS AND LAMB STEAKS

Thickness	Minutes per side, at medium heat: 350° Rare	Minutes per side, after searing at 500°, then reducing flame to 350° Medium
1 inch	6	4–5
1½ inch	9	6–7
2 inch	11	8–10

PORK CHOPS AND STEAKS
(Must be cooked until juice is clear)

Thickness	Minutes per side
⅓ inch	2
½ inch	3
¾ inch	4

HAM SLICES
(Precooked ham, broiled at 400°–450°)

Thickness	Minutes per side
⅓ inch	3–4
½ inch	5–6
¾ inch	7–8
1	10–12

TECHNIQUES OF BROILING FOWL

Chicken should first be coated with a combination of melted butter, salt, and pepper before broiling. A marinade sauce or more butter should be brushed on throughout the process. Place chicken at least 5 inches from the flame, setting it on a greased rack or trivet. Start the cooking with the bone side up, then reverse it, coat it thoroughly with the same mixture, and continue to brush it frequently with the sauce or butter. The total broiling time is about 25 minutes, and doneness can be judged by piercing the second joint to see that the juice runs clear.

For young turkey the same rules apply as for broiling chicken, but the cooking time will generally be about 10 minutes longer.

TECHNIQUES OF BROILING FISH FILLETS AND STEAKS

Even "fatty" fish isn't very fatty. In order not to produce something with the texture and flavor of blotting paper, therefore, you must coat fish fillets and steaks very thoroughly with butter (*not* margarine, for it won't stand up to broiling heat). Keep plenty of butter at hand, or a mixture of butter and oil, or a marinade with which to coat the fish frequently as it cooks.

Place fish on a greased grill or trivet about 4 inches from a medium flame. Cook 5 to 8 minutes on one side, then (after being sure it is well coated with butter or a mixture of butter and oil) reverse and cook it on the other side for an identical period.

Fish should be flaky when thoroughly broiled.

TECHNIQUES OF BROILING LOBSTER

These are usually broiled "live," as the term is. Actually, this involves cutting the creature in half while it is alive—a grizzly business, I'm afraid, but quickly done. Lay the crustacean on its back, piercing it between the eyes with a strong, sharp knife. This strikes the brain, occasioning instant death, though it will wiggle a bit afterward, which can be somewhat unnerving.

After being coated with butter, salt, and pepper, lobster should be cooked at medium heat with the meat side up, until the meat of the underside of the tail is opaque. Keep basting it regularly to be sure the meat retains its moisture.

PANBROILING

Panbroiling is a rapid and efficient method of cooking thin slices of meat. The essence of the process is searing the surface of the cut to prevent the juices from escaping. The pan employed is a skillet, preferably of cast iron, brought to a high temperature before the meat is introduced. The only material to be added is a generous sprinkling of salt (kosher salt crystals are ideal) which prevents the meat from sticking to the surface.

Do not add grease to the skillet. The high heat you'll be applying in the panbroiling process will burn all animal fats and clarified butter; olive oil will impart a flavor you don't want. As for the safety of the utensil itself, there is no need for worry when you're using a good iron skillet. It can take the heat! Just reseason according to manufacturer's directions every 4 to 6 months, depending on use.

Place the meat on the skillet and turn it when the beads of juice have just begun to rise to the upper surface. After the second side has been well seared, turn the heat down a little.

If the meat is firm but elastic to a touch of your finger, it is sufficiently cooked. (Touch a piece of raw meat to determine the difference.) A little experience will teach you when the cut has reached the precise state you prefer—rare, medium, etc. When you're panbroiling a cube steak, for example, the procedure is almost instantaneous. One, two, three, and it's done.

Note: If your meat or pan should catch fire, throw on handfuls of salt to put out the flame. Sometimes the meat is salvageable, otherwise open a can with a smile.

DUTCH-OVEN PORK CHOPS

My favorite way to cook pork chops is in a Dutch oven. I salt and pepper them vigorously, heat some butter in the Dutch oven, lightly brown the chops on both sides, put on the lid, then turn down the heat and cook them 5 or 10 minutes, depending on their thickness. These steamed chops are, I think, preferable to boiled ones.

SPIT-ROASTING

One of the most ancient methods of cooking, and certainly one of the oldest methods of roasting, is spit-roasting; that is, the placing of a roast or a fowl on a skewer which is fixed to a rack near a source of heat—whether it be a special attachment to your stove, an electric or charcoal-fired rotisserie, or the fireplace described below.

When humans had mastered fire, they doubtless first heated meat over its flames. With developing civilization, our ancestors built spits into their hearths. Each member of the family or its servants took a turn at revolving the roast. It was a hot and sometimes a strenuous task, for some spits could accommodate the entire carcass of a pretty large creature, wild or domesticated.

In our own more technologically sophisticated era, someone devised the charcoal grill and the electric rotisserie. There are also clockwork roasters that are used in fireplaces, but I've only seen them in Europe, where the antique and modern methods are still occasionally to be seen in startling juxtaposition. Nowhere in the world, I think, can there be a more awesome culinary sight than the cavernous but architecturally splendid kitchens of the great medieval French monastery of Fontevrault-l'Abbaye. They feature twenty enormous hearths. It makes the mind of the most ardent cook boggle to contemplate those vast fireplaces in simultaneous operation.

Fire Suitable for Spit-Roasting
As with the various types of broiler available, so you should be guided in the employment of rotisseries by the instructions furnished. Charcoal or wood *embers* are the preferable fuels, because they enhance the flavor of the meat roasted. If you have difficulties getting that sort of fire to the suitable state where your live coals are covered with a gray ash or your wood is well charred, you might try a rather alarming-looking method my husband deploys on such occasions: He reverses the hose of a tank-type vacuum cleaner and plays the air discreetly over the coals until they are just right. This should only be attempted in a spot where there is no fire hazard. He used to use kerosene or gasoline, to which I put a stop, because I could taste the fumes of these petroleum compounds in the roast. *All* these products occasion that danger. You must be sure that all the petroleum residues have been burned away before you roast.

A rather special variant is used by a man I know: a small riveter's stove with a hand-cranked fan.

Techniques of Spit-Roasting
The closeness to the heat of the material to be roasted is dependent on the size and nature of the cut. Most people place pieces like steak on a rack or trivet; others I know simply throw it right on the coals, something I've never had the courage to do.

Red meat should first be browned before being subjected to a high, penetrating heat. The fire should be as hot as manageable without actually flaming. As for charcoal broiling, so for spit-roasting; the flames can be controlled by dampening the embers gingerly with a garden watering can.

White meat requires a lower temperature in order to allow the flesh to brown and cook at the same time. The instructions are the same as for broiling, as noted earlier.

Small fowl *do* require open flames, not merely glowing embers.

When you are spit-roasting you must baste constantly, and the piece you are preparing should be very thoroughly barded before you begin. For basting, you may use oil, butter, a delicious marinade, barbecue sauce, or just the juices that accumulate in the pan if you're using an electric rotisserie. Use a bristle or feather brush for this purpose.

Timing for Spit-Roasting

The time required for spit-roasting is roughly comparable to your own oven timings for a similar cut, though charcoal embers make such pinpoint accuracy of estimates impossible. As with panbroiling, the dish is done when it is firm to the touch or the juices run clear.

If you feel you've *got* to have a peek at the cooking meat, accomplish this with a very sharp-pointed knife, making as tiny an incision as you can manage. If you are roasting a bird, pierce the thigh. If the juice emerging is clear, the fowl is cooked.

Cuts of Meat for Spit-Roasting

Consult the earlier portion of this chapter dealing with cuts suitable for regular roasting (p. 16). Essentially, these are identical.

The Good and the Bad News About Spit-Roasting

Spit-roasting has one major practical disadvantage. Of all such methods of preparation, it is the most wasteful by a wide margin, for it occasions the greatest amount of shrinkage. For some cooks, however, the involvement, the attention required, the resulting flavor, and the warmth of the fire—not to mention the occasionally spectacular flaring of the flame—make up for that drawback. And you're always able to see what you're doing.

CARVING

Now that we have prepared the meat, it seems appropriate to say something about serving it, i.e., carving. I was brought up in (and retain) the European tradition which holds that it is the woman of the house who does the carving. I am now very good at it. There's undoubtedly some profound significance, having to do with war and peace, that accounts for the tradition that it is the man in the family who does the carving. It probably goes back to the good old days when men killed each other individually with spears and swords, and thus were presumed skillful in the lowlier arts of carving the Sunday roast. Without indulging myself in sociological speculation of this sort, I must observe that most butchers are men, and that good butchers always use knives that they are constantly sharpening. John Verdery, headmaster of Wooster School, is the most skilled carver of my acquaintance. He learned this craft from his grandfather, and along with it came the counsel that one should always carve in a way that leaves half of the object sliced for use the next day. His grandfather called the other half the "wooden side." I'm not sure I'm in sympathy with this admonition, but John's talent is dazzling, and since my husband is helpless in this respect, I always ask John to carve when he and his wife dine with us. It's a delight to see him at his work. He says that the essence of carving is the sharpness of the knife. As a general observation, it might be added that most kitchen tasks requiring knives are more swiftly *and* more safely accomplished with a sharp instrument than with a dull one. A knowledge of a given creature's anatomy is helpful, too. Details may be found in *The Art of Carving*, Simon and Schuster.

2

Compound Subjects:
Deep Frying,
Panfrying,
Sautéing

An Unexpected Treat

Some years ago my husband and I were at Tours, in the Loire valley. We had just an hour for lunch, which is not nearly adequate time for that meal under most respectable circumstances in France. So we imagined that we would have to settle for nourishment without very much pleasure. Since we found ourselves near the great cathedral, and since all the restaurants recommended by the usually reliable *Guide Michelin* were some distance away from that section of the city, we had no choice but to take our chances with the fare offered by one of the small cafés near at hand. Although we are congenital browsers when we're traveling, we walked quickly now because we were starved (French breakfasts being humble repasts, at best). The first restaurant we came upon was in a *sous-sol,* a few steps down from the sidewalk. It didn't appear especially inviting, but we entered anyhow. The *propriétaire* handed us a skimpy, hand-written menu composed in the inevitable violet ink. The range of possibilities was certainly less than grand, but the prices were decidedly reasonable! I forget the cost for a *prix fixe* lunch, and I'm sure that the figure I remember so vividly is an exaggeration of the fact, but it was very inexpensive.

At that point, pressed for time and extremely hungry, we opted for what was ready. The first course was promptly served. It turned out to be an absolutely delicious *friture de la Loire,* and suddenly we were rejoicing in a gratifying sensation of complacency—the one-upman's feeling of having discovered a genuine bargain. My God, and it *was* delicious, too! *Friture de la Loire,* as presented in that modest, almost self-effacing restaurant near the cathedral of Tours, was a platter of tiny river fish (all of them smaller than one's little finger), flawlessly fried in deep fat, sprinkled with parsley, and served with a quarter of lemon on the side. I can taste it once again even as I'm writing about it, and wish that I had an identical plateful before me right now.

DEEP FRYING

I think most cooks have predilections for certain modes of preparation—roasting, broiling, casseroles, etc. Deep frying, perhaps, offers the widest range of opportunities in the preparation of dishes, many of them very inexpensive, whether as a first course, main course, or dessert. If you have in your kitchen all of the principal ingredients, and are interested in widening your culinary horizons, deep frying can produce very satisfying results. You may also become adept at frying and thus come really to take pleasure in it, if you've not experimented with the process before.

I've discussed elsewhere the various dry-heat methods of preparing meat, fowl, and fish. This chapter is devoted to the use of fats and oils as the mediums by which heat is conveyed to the food cooked. Where hot air or a hot surface transmits the heat in the other techniques, the temperature of various heated materials—lard, butter, margarine, olive oil or the other vegetable oils—has a quite different effect in the processes of deep frying, panfrying, and sautéing. In deep frying the food is literally boiled in oil, which forms a crust on the surface and then transfers heat very rapidly and intensely to the center.

It is terribly useful to be able to prepare such a wide variety of cheese, meat, fish, vegetable, and dessert dishes—not to overlook that great and universally popular weakness, French fried potatoes, which, if properly done, are far superior, when homemade, to the frozen packages we choose out of indolence.

Equipment

The first requirement for any sort of frying is adequate ventilation. You really ought to have a powerful exhaust fan if you fry extensively. If you're not so provided, *you* as the cook may be able to abide the smoke and the fumes, but the rest of your household is usually more reluctant to put up with them.

For deep frying, it's best to have a special fryer, that is, a container specifically designed for the purpose. It is quite deep, as the name suggests, and is equipped with a heavy wire basket that can be lowered into and raised out of the hot oil or fat. It also has a rack on its edge to hold the basket above the hot liquid as it drains.

You may also need a perforated skimmer which allows the oil to filter off as you remove the food you are cooking from the fryer.

A frying and sugar syrup thermometer is really a must for deep frying, since it will give you the most reliable guide to proper frying temperatures, which can, at times, be critical to success. However, in a pinch, you can drop pieces of fresh bread into the hot oil or fat; by the speed with which they turn brown, you can make a rough determination of the heat. I confess that this procedure makes *me* nervous. Besides, you can make other important culinary uses of your thermometer, as in the making of frostings and jams and jellies.

Another essential is a fine-meshed sieve with which to strain the fat or oil after you are through using it.

Finally, you should have a heat-proof container in which to store the cooking oil or grease between uses.

Frying Mediums

The following products may be employed for deep frying:

Animal fats (which you can prepare yourself
  —see "Rendering," below)
Lard
Vegetable fats
Olive oil
Corn or peanut oil

All the experts are agreed that you *must* use some kind of oil for the frying of fish. Oil is also required when you want to attain the highest possible frying temperatures. Other fats cannot be brought to heat sufficiently high without burning and scorching. That is, they begin to scorch before they are hot enough to do the job demanded.

Rendering

If you find that you are doing a great deal of deep frying, it will be well worth your time and effort to prepare your own frying mixture—to "render" your own grease, the term used to describe the refinement of raw animal fat. Though this medium does impose certain limitations on degree of heat attainable, its utility and economy merit a description of the rendering process.

Obtain from your butcher 2 pounds of beef kidney fat (suet). It *must* be kidney fat. In addition, you should purchase a pound of veal kidney fat and a pound of pork kidney fat (or a pound of lard).

You *can* make your own frying mixture entirely of beef kidney fat, in which event you will need 4 pounds.

Cut all the different kinds of fat into small pieces and place them in a deep, heavy pot—preferably cast iron. Cover them completely with water. Cook them slowly until all the water has evaporated, by which time the small pieces of nonfatty tissue will be crisp and free of fat. When this preparation begins to emit a bluish smoke, it has been totally rendered.

Allow the melted material to cool for 20 minutes before straining it through a very fine-meshed sieve or a piece of muslin. As a matter of course, it is useful to have a yard or two of muslin (which you've thoroughly washed) and some cheesecloth in one of your kitchen drawers. They're often needed.

Put the strained fat back into the pot and reheat it, adding to it two large onions, thinly sliced. Cook until the onions are dancing on the surface of the boiling fat. By this time, your rendered fat is ready for use. Strain again.

It will remain in good condition for a surprisingly long time. Always allow it to cool for 20 minutes before attempting to cope with it, and always remember to strain it after each use before returning it to its storage container (which must not be of plastic). This rendered fat may be safely heated to the same temperature attained with lard (see table, p. 42).

Techniques of Deep Frying

You must give your frying mixture enough time to achieve its proper temperature before introducing the objects to be fried in it. This will require 20 minutes or so, depending on the speed of your stove. If the fat is too cool when you start to fry in it, the foods you are preparing will become impregnated with the fat and they will taste dreadful.

Never try to fry too many pieces at one time. Fry in very modest batches.

Never fill your fryer more than halfway to the top with the

grease. The fat bubbles furiously when the food is immersed in it, and an overfull fryer will cause a terrible mess on your stove—at best. At worst, it constitutes a serious fire hazard.

Food for frying should be at room temperature when it is placed in deep fat. Don't attempt to fry objects coming straight from your freezer or even from your refrigerator. Be sure as well that the surfaces of the food are dry. Once the pieces have been fully fried, they must be placed on some sort of highly absorbent material which will soak up the surplus fat that drains off. Heavy brown paper is best. Tear open a shopping bag, or use several thicknesses of paper toweling for the purpose. Keep the fried food warm in the oven with the door open.

Deep-Fat Temperatures

Butter: 248°
Clarified butter: 269°–275° (see p. 45 for explanation of and directions for clarifying butter)
Animal fats: Moderately hot   275°–284°
               Hot   320°
               Very hot   356° (smoking slightly)
Lard and rendered fat: 392°
Vegetable fat: 482°
Peanut and corn oils: 518°
Olive oil: 554°

The temperature at which you fry will depend on what you are frying, and also on whether you are cooking something from a raw state (i.e., cooking it completely in a single stage) or merely heating it through, as with a fritter, for example. Another factor determining the suitable temperature is the size of the pieces to be fried. The rule cited for broiling is applicable to frying as well: the smaller the piece, the higher the temperature.

Foods which naturally contain a lot of moisture (vegetables, fruits, and fish, for instance) will require the maximum heat to be attained with animal fat: 356°. This gives them a chance to cook thoroughly before the outer crust becomes too brown.

Foods like fritters and croquettes—precooked items that must be heated through, rather than actually cooked, to make them palatable—demand a higher temperature: 385°. This is called for because you need to seal a crust of batter and bread crumbs immediately.

Small fish, cheese tidbits, and other little pieces that you want to cook through rapidly require a heat of about 390°.

PANFRYING AND SAUTÉING

I propose to discuss these two processes together because, while they are slightly different from each other, separate descriptions suggest distinctions that are both arbitrary and possibly misleading. "Panfry" is the British and American term for food prepared in a special kind of utensil—the frying pan or skillet, a vessel with low, flared sides that encourage the dispersion of vapors during the cooking process. The medium is fat, the amount to be employed varying considerably, according to the material being prepared. It is possible to accomplish small amounts of deep frying as well as panfrying in a skillet.

Sauté is the past participle of the French verb "to jump" or "to leap." The expression in cooking derives from the possibility (if you happen to be interested in culinary spectaculars) of flipping the contents of a pan with a single deft motion of your wrist. The object involved makes a 180-degree turn in the air and lands back in the pan on its opposite side.

In my own mind, the term "sauté" is associated with a cooking procedure that calls for motion, moving the food about considerably, either turning it over frequently or stirring it with regularity.

Panfrying will vary in method from the preparation of fried chicken, fish, or *Wienerschnitzel*, which require much fat of the same sort employed in deep-fat frying—the utensil half full of very hot grease—to frying an egg, which needs very little fat.

For panfrying, a mixture of half butter and half vegetable oil or olive oil is often an excellent medium, since this blend has a greater tolerance for higher temperatures than butter alone. Pure butter is best for such things as French toast or delicate fish (clarified butter is best of all), wherever its fragile flavor will enhance the dish. Never try to use margarine as a substitute for butter in this kind of frying. It will separate and scorch unless great care is taken, even at fairly low temperatures. When the flavor of it harmonizes well with the material being prepared, bacon fat is useful for frying.

Panfrying and sautéing are distinct modes of cooking in themselves. Sautéing has another, equally important, role in cooking, for it is often a first step in the preparation of meat and vegetables to be used in the making of soups and stews —combination cooking. You'll discover as you proceed through this volume that I refer with great frequency to the sautéing process as a step complementary even to roasting. In this application the object is not to cook completely, but to brown or sear meats, to brown or "sweat" vegetables —that is, to cook until they are soft and give off their own juices—that are to be further cooked in another way.

What's the Difference Betweeen Frying and Sautéing?

The essential difference between the processes of frying and sautéing lies in the amount of fat employed—generally less of it in the latter. This, however, is not invariably so. In sautéing vegetables, for example, a good deal of butter, oil, or fat may be required because you wish to avoid browning them; it's a question of personal taste.

Clarified Butter

When it is appropriate to use butter alone for frying, it is worth going to the trouble of clarifying it, thereby increasing its heat capacity appreciably. For this purpose either sweet or salted butter may be used. I prefer sweet butter under all circumstances.

Place the butter in a small saucepan and melt it at low heat. A whitish froth will come to the surface. Carefully skim this off.

When the butter is melted, slowly pour it into another container. I use a heat-resistant glass so that I can see, while I'm pouring it out of that container, when I reach the milky residue at the bottom. This sediment is *not* to be transferred.

Breading

Food which is to be panfried or sautéed as its sole method of preparation is often breaded—dipped first in milk and then flour and bread crumbs. When a special recipe is used, such as southern-style fried chicken (which is dipped first in milk and then in flour mixed with salt and pepper), I usually add cayenne pepper. You should also flour fish, liver, and other foods that will disintegrate, to help bind them together—and also to form a crust that will retain the natural juices and flavor during the frying or sautéing. To the mixture in which I place foods such as soft-shelled crabs, I add a little crushed garlic. If you wish, you may also introduce some herb you think appropriate to the dish you are preparing.

For breading, first dip the food into a mixture of beaten egg flavored with a small amount of oil, water, or milk (the recipe will specify which ingredient), to which has been added salt, pepper, garlic, and herbs (if you wish).

Roll each item in unflavored bread crumbs (or crumbs flavored with those herbs and spices you prefer). I find it preferable to prepare my own bread crumbs. I crush stale bread with a beautiful heavy round rock picked up on an ocean beach. The ready-to-use variety of crumbs always seems to me to have a tendency to be tasteless. I eschew the preflavored kind; for some reason, the commercial seasonings taste "off" and flat to me.

Equipment

The purist requires a proper pan for the sauté method. This is a straight-sided skillet, usually made of tin-lined copper or heavy aluminum.

The frying pan, like the sautéing pan, should be of heavy metal. The old-fashioned cast-iron skillet is impossible to improve on. Those of lighter materials, even the thickest aluminum, will soon become warped or deformed by the intense heat you must occasionally expose them to.

The other requirements for panfrying and sautéing are a pair of tongs, a pancake turner, a slotted or perforated metal spoon, and wooden spoons for stirring. In time, one establishes a special affection for a particular wooden spoon—as its edges wear down to conform to your personal style of stirring.

Techniques of Panfrying and Sautéing

The size of your frying pan or sautéing pan should be determined by the quantity of food you're preparing—large enough to accommodate the food and to allow you ample room for turning it over and/or stirring it, but small enough to conserve the amount of grease you use. It is preferable to use two small pans or to cook in batches, rather than to overcrowd a single utensil. Overcrowding, in addition to its inconvenience, impairs the browning process and prevents the uniform cooking of each object, since it prevents the ready diffusion of the heat and lowers it as well. A pan that is too large makes it possible to burn at the same time both the food and the bottom of the utensil.

The heat to be applied is highly variable, depending on the dish you're preparing. Employ high temperature when you are more concerned with browning the food and forming a crust than with cooking it thoroughly. *Always lower the heat to complete the cooking process.*

It is seldom necessary to place a lid on a pan used for frying. As in the case of roasting, the effect of this is to steam the food. However, some cooks prefer the flavor of fried food which has been steamed during the final stages of preparation—like potatoes, onions, mushrooms, or pork chops. I always cover my pork chops.

Use of Sautéing in Sauces and Before Other Processes

I'm an extremely heterodox cook, occasionally a heretical one, and frequently dogmatic in the bargain.

To be dogmatic, for the moment, let me state my absolute conviction that if you wish to make a first-rate casserole or a fine stew, you should first brown the meat to be used. That is, it should be sautéed, but not cooked through, in a little fat before being placed in a casserole or stewing pot. The reason for sautéing the meat before putting it into the pot is to prevent the juices from draining too quickly, thus causing a loss of flavor in the small pieces you've cut up. Another reason is to keep the meat from disintegrating during the long stewing process.

Vegetables should also be sautéed, and all the juices accumulated in the pan ought to be poured into the pot or casserole.

The time involved in taking these extra steps is no more than 15 or 20 minutes, a measure of the difference between caring a great deal about the quality of the dish you are making and not caring very much—which isn't enough. I can't emphasize sufficiently that as far as I'm concerned, this is time well invested.

Sautéing as a Base for Sauces

When you plan to cook something completely by sautéing it, you can make a most delicious sauce immediately after the cooking is completed by rinsing the sautéing pan with wine or stock. You may also add some mustard or herbs of your choice with shallots, and stir them in with the residual juices from the sautéing process.

To sauté is a great way of cooking a dish that has real individual character when your time is limited.

Foods Suitable for Panfrying or Sautéing

BEEF
  Cube steaks
  Liver
  Thin slices of beef
  Lean hamburger

LAMB
  Steaks
  Rib chops
  Frenched chops
  Shoulder chops
  Saratoga chops
  Loin chops
  Blade chops
  English chops
  Patties
  Kidneys
  Liver

VEAL
  Loin chops
  Sirloin steaks
  Kidney chops
  Rib chops
  Scallops
  Rosettes
  Mock chicken legs
  Patties
  Liver

PORK
  Tenderloin
  Canadian bacon
  Loin chops
  Rib chops
  Frenched rib chops
  Butterfly chops
  Ham slices
  Bacon
  Liver
  Kidneys

FOWL
  Frying chickens
  Turkey breasts

FISH
  Small fish (fingerlings)
  Steaks and fillets of larger fish (salmon, swordfish, bluefish, halibut, tuna, cod, sole, etc.)
  Soft-shelled crabs

VEGETABLES
  Onions
  Potatoes
  Eggplants
  Tomatoes
  Peppers—all types
  Spinach
  Squashes

3

The Adjectival Clause: Stocks, *Courts Bouillons,* *Fumets*

Embellishing the Dish

Because so many major recipes are predicated on them, every cook should have a personal repertory of stocks to serve as the base for soups and casseroles, for poaching, and for the cooking of fish dishes.

Before describing the techniques involved in the preparation of meat, fish, and poultry in liquids, and the methods referred to as "combination cooking" (i.e., braising, fricasseeing, pot roasting, and poaching), I think it necessary first to discuss the contents of the liquids used in these processes and the means of making them They are called stocks, *courts bouillons,* and *fumets* (with seafood).

STOCKS

Stocks form the essential ingredients for consommés, some soups, and most sauces.

A stock is produced with the flesh and bones of meat, fowl, or fish, to which are added vegetables described as "aromatic" (onion, carrot, leek, parsnip, turnip, and celery) and selected herbs and spices. The liquid vehicle may be wine, vinegar, or plain water. The basic and the spicy materials will depend in part on the purpose you intend. I recommend that you sample various recipes until you discover the stocks whose flavor you like best.

Many cooks don't take the trouble to make their own stock because they imagine it to be too expensive as well as too time-consuming. With respect to the time (anywhere from 2 to 8 hours), it should be noted that you don't have to watch the stock while it's simmering away. And as for the expense, I note a bit later that from a *pot au feu* you can obtain three complete meals. To a lesser extent, the same may be said of other stocks, too.

I use the meats that survive the preparation of brown and white stocks to make salads, croquettes, or hash. Moreover, the meats employed are, to begin with, of the very cheapest variety, the sort you'd buy *only* for the manufacture of stock, for it takes this amount of simmering to make such pieces chewable. Yet their flavor is still delicious, even after they've given much of it to the stock. Until you've made the attempt, you'll just have to take this on faith.

In addition to the salvaging of meats left over from the preparation of stock, I also save the vegetables, especially the carrots, and serve them in salads. Consequently, the byproducts of the stockmaking are by no means insignificant.

If you require further persuasion, I suggest that you simply multiply the number of cans of quality beef or chicken consommé needed to make a gallon and add up the sum expended!

I plan ahead when I know that I need or wish to make more chicken stock. I save the carcasses and other bones of chicken already used in other dishes, thus economizing on the wings, backs, and necks it is necessary to purchase. If this practice should impress you as less than perfectly sanitary, bear in mind that the reused bones are to be boiled for hours, so there's not the slightest danger of contamination —assuming, of course, that you've kept your flotsam and jetsam fresh by cold storage or freezing. Once the stock is made, I separate the solids from the fluid and I pick over the chicken bones and use the rescued meat to make salad, croquettes, hash, creamed chicken, or stuffing for avocado. The pieces of meat thus gleaned aren't particularly elegant in appearance, but they're exceptionally tasty and make perfectly satisfactory family fare.

If you're not planning to eat the vegetables after you've used them to prepare stock, you need not peel them before putting them in the stock pot. Just clean them thoroughly, slice them up with a paring knife, and put them in the cauldron. In any case, you should add an unpeeled yellow onion to the mixture to improve the color of your stock.

The meats and bones and vegetables and spices are cooked in water over a very low, simmering heat until virtually all their flavors and essences have been extracted and allowed to blend.

Uses of Stocks

There are some instances where you may employ plain water for cooking, as in the preparation of stews. But initially, at least, you'll have to take it on faith again that stock will enormously enhance the flavor of any dish where the introduction of water is appropriate. You should use stock and/or wine in the making of all casseroles and dishes to be braised—though you *may* substitute canned broth or dehydrated beef or chicken cubes. I've found myself, although as rarely as possible, caught without a stock on hand, and I've always been furious—because the canned or dried substitutes just aren't to be compared with the original homemade product.

If you really care about the quality of your cooking you'll surely want to manufacture your own stock, instead of having to resort to the miserably bland or desiccated alternatives. It's entirely a question of cultivating the habit. Please heed!

For the person who has a reasonably large freezer, there's really no plausible excuse for not taking the time to prepare stocks. They freeze admirably, and thus can be readied whenever you require them. Stock will also keep for relatively long periods in your refrigerator, *provided* that you remember to bring them to a boil for about 10 minutes every two or three days. I have to concede, however, that this can be a damned nuisance. In this connection, a friend of mine, Mary Carter Jones, passed on an excellent tip from Dorothy Rodgers, who writes so well on topics of household elegance. Mrs. Rodgers fills ice-cube trays with stock and stores them in her freezer. In this way she's always got small quantities available when she needs them.

Types of Stocks

The most useful stocks for general purposes are brown stock and chicken stock. Another is white stock, which I make only when I require it for a specific dish, such as the gelatin for a *pâté* or some very special recipe that calls for the use of white stock.

While most stocks require quite a lot of time to prepare, fish stock may be made just before you have a need for it, because it is ready for use about 20 minutes after it has come to a boil. It may, however, be prepared ahead and stored in your freezer. The point is that it can be made in literally the time it takes to do the preliminary work on the dish in which you are going to use it.

A *pot au feu*, as I've observed, is a doubly or even trebly useful recipe, for it furnishes you with at least two complete meals, in addition to the stock which is a by-product of its preparation.

BROWN STOCK

Brown stock is made with the meat of a shank of beef, the leg bone itself, a piece of the cheapest beef you can find, veal knuckle bones, a piece of bacon rind or a slab of salted pigskin, a ham bone (if available), and the aromatic vegetables and herbs called for in the recipe, which I described at the beginning of the chapter.

Brown stock is the best of all for general use. You'll often find that in employing it, you can thin it down with water or wine to make it go farther. Since its preparation requires a good deal of time, as noted, you might as well make at least a gallon of it on each occasion (which means that you'll start out with about twice that amount). It requires about 8 hours to prepare.

Since I used to hold down a job as well as being a housewife, I found it most convenient to make my brown stock on Sundays. I don't like leaving my cooking utterly without attention, and it pleases me to poke and stir and sniff as the stock progresses. It gives me a feeling of total involvement which is one of the great joys of concerned cooking.

CHICKEN STOCK

Chicken stock for home use is simple to make if, as I've remarked, you've prudently conserved carcasses, hearts, and gizzards. In addition to this accumulation from my freezer, I usually purchase necks, wings, and backs (often sold separately at low prices, especially in supermarkets). It really doesn't much matter which chicken parts you use—the cheaper the better, so long as they're fresh. I also put into my chicken stock a piece of salt pork (after it has been blanched—simmered in water for 3 or 4 minutes to remove the excess of grease and the coating of old salt).

Odd as it may seem, a chicken stock is appreciably improved by the introduction of veal bones.

Finally, you add the aromatic vegetables, herbs, and spices.

It takes between 2 and 3 hours to make chicken stock. I find it most provident of my time to make it while I'm preparing an evening meal and cleaning up after it. The stock is finished cooking at just about the time I'm ready for bed.

WHITE STOCK

White stock is composed of the usual aromatic vegetables and seasonings combined with veal, veal bones, and chicken giblets which you may have preserved or purchased. The cooking time is about 4 hours.

Planning Your Time for Making Stocks

Preparing good stocks doesn't require massive amounts of effort, but (with the exception of fish stock) it *does* take a lot of time. With a little planning, however, you won't feel that you've had to exert yourself excessively, and the results are more than worth the hours and labor expended.

When I'm preparing a chicken stock or a white stock, I try to time it so that I'm able to drain the stock pot just before going to bed, thus allowing it to cool overnight. Then, the following morning, I place it in the refrigerator. When I return home that evening, I skim the fat off the chilled surface, then boil the stock up once more for at least 10 minutes to sterilize it before decanting it into containers for storage.

Those gallon or larger-sized plastic juice containers are ideal for cooling and degreasing stock. Since their necks have a small diameter, the fat forms in a nice thick cake on top and is easy to remove.

Equipment

The first and most important requisite for making stock is a large pot, one with a minimum capacity of 2 gallons. (This utensil will also be useful for other operations, like making big batches of spaghetti.) You also need a bowl of equal volume.

Another requirement is a big colander. Perfectly satisfactory alternatives are a large fine-meshed sieve, or a piece of muslin or cheesecloth, or even a portion of wornout sheet, well rinsed. Not only do you want to strain your stock, but you'll want it as free as possible of loose particles—extremely clear.

You should have a long-handled wooden spoon for stirring and, if you can find one, a blunt-ended spoon or scoop for skimming.

You will also need storage containers. Plastic canisters or some other frost-proof and leak-proof vessels ought to be used if you are planning to freeze your stock.

Techniques of Making Stocks

Fish and chicken bones need no advance preparation. The bones of veal and beef, however, should be roasted in a 400° oven until they achieve a shade of pale brown before being placed in your stock pot. This helps to reduce the amount of skimming later on, and it will enhance the flavor and color of the stock as well.

When you're preparing a brown stock, you should sauté the cut-up vegetables in beef drippings before contributing them to the pot.

Always start the preparation of any stock in cold water. Use high heat to bring it to a boil, then reduce the temperature to a low simmer and keep skimming the surface as the foam rises. *Stock should never be allowed to boil while it is cooking.* Just let it simmer for the time required, depending on the type you're making. Boiling is done to reduce the stock after it has matured.

I don't use a lid while making stock.

STRAINING

After the stock has been thoroughly cooked, it requires very careful straining. For general purposes, you don't need to clarify it (see below). Just strain it completely. Then allow it to cool.

Once it is cooled, all the fat which has more or less solidified on the surface must be meticulously removed—a delicate operation that I greatly enjoy, though it demands some patience. The final residue of fat is best taken off the surface of the stock with the tip of a folded paper towel.

If you've made so much stock that your colander can't accommodate all the bones and vegetables that have to be separated from the liquid, there is a method of coping with the situation. I'm indebted to Elizabeth David's excellent *French Provincial Cooking* for this tip: Find a stool or chair, one whose bottom has a seat large enough to hold the bowl into which you are going to pour out your stock. Reverse the stool on a table and place the bowl on the upturned seat. Then secure the four corners of a square of muslin or cheesecloth or sheeting to the legs to form a bag. Gradually pour the contents of the stock pot into this pocket you have made, thus perfectly straining it. It is doubtless easier to purchase a larger colander, especially if you make stock fairly regularly. It is a useful investment, since you can also strain other dishes, such as large (or small) quantities of pasta, and use it to rinse fruit and salads.

CLARIFYING STOCKS

When making use of your stock as the base for jellied soups or for gelatin dishes, you may have to spend the extra time and money to clarify it—that is, to remove *all* its impurities—so that you wind up with a fluid that's crystal clear.

What you will need in order to clarify the stock is at least a pound of lean hamburger and the white of an egg. They serve as magnets for the loose particles in the stock which, in consequence, cling to them when the fluid is strained. The amounts of each substance required will obviously depend on the quantity of stock to be clarified. (Consult your favorite recipe for these details.)

Bring the stock to a boil. Then add the raw egg white and hamburger and bring it to a boil once again, stirring it a few times just after it has begun to boil. When it has been boiling briskly for 3 or 4 minutes, let it set for 10 minutes, then strain off the hamburger, using a very fine sieve or cloth. The salvaged meat will be of interest only to a pet that will eat anything.

REDUCING STOCKS

With clarified stock, you can make wonderful jellies and aspics. These are produced by *reducing* the clarified stock.

If your stock is endowed with enough of its own gelatinous material (much of it derived from the marrow of the bones you've used in its preparation), you'll not have to add powdered gelatin to the mixture. The instructions on packets of gelatin will give you the proper proportions of powder to liquid. It is by taste that you determine when the stock, reduced by boiling, is sufficiently evaporated for your purpose. And as with jelly, you may test the product in the same way you would a sweet preserve—by examining to see that it coats the surface of a spoon, or maintains its jellied consistency when a drop of the hot liquid is plopped into a cup of chilled water.

It's simply not possible to suggest a precise length of time for this operation, because the amount of heat and the quantity of stock to be reduced are critically important variables. You should, at all events, allow at least an hour.

GLACE DE VIANDE

By very nearly boiling away a clarified brown stock, you'll create *glace de viande,* a precious jellied elixir, the ambergris of the kitchen, which will keep literally for months in your refrigerator. One tablespoon of *glace de viande* stirred into a sautéing pan with a little wine makes a simple, supremely elegant, and unforgettably delicious sauce.

COURTS BOUILLONS

Court bouillon is an elegant name for stock. As the term implies, it is cooked for less time than a stock to be used for a clear soup. You can use a stock for a *court bouillon,* but you cannot reverse the procedure.

FUMETS

Fumet is the name of the fish stock equivalent of a *court bouillon*. It is prepared in 20 minutes.

MEAGER STOCKS (STOCKS MADE WITH LEFTOVERS)

It is the impression of many cooks that a French stock pot is something of a catchall, sitting on the "warm," day in and day out, receiving bits and pieces, and returning a delicious broth to the thrifty French housewife. This is largely a fiction comparable to someone coming back from a trip to Appalachia with tales of a "magic" stock pot.

These pots are full of poverty. That doesn't mean that you can't make use of leftover bones; a small amount of broth can be produced by boiling up the bones of almost any kind of meat, provided that you make sure to add fresh aromatic vegetables and herbs (eschewing, please, those expensive packages of desiccated products advertised as "soup" components) and that you give the preparation the same sort of care you'd offer to a richer stock. You must remember, however, that in making a meager stock you should use much less water at the outset, for most of the vitality and flavor of the bones will have been taken away from them in their previous cooking. It's a case of second best being better than nothing. Bearing this in mind, you'll find a meager stock useful, especially in making fowl and lamb dishes.

There is a final trick to be accomplished with the remains of your own original stock, if you have a large freezer. After you have made your stock and shriven the bones of all their meat, place them in a pot, cover them generously with cold water, and boil them up again for a couple of hours. You can do this the day after you've finished making your stock, provided that you refrigerate the bones in the meantime.

The purpose of this exercise is to make a fluid which you subsequently freeze. It will provide you with an excellent head start as the base for the next batch of stock you prepare. It will improve the flavor of your new stock because it has more flavor than the plain tap water with which you'd normally begin.

I implore you to renounce recourse to the can and the cube, to turn to the frequent use of the stock pot. It is a rewarding habit to acquire.

4

The Run-on Sentence: *Cooking in Liquids*

Crisis in the Kitchen

Years ago, when Donald and I lived the year-round in East Hampton, near the end of Long Island, we were able in the winter to take advantage of some rare opportunities provided by this proximity to the sea and the fishing industry. Deep-sea trawlers would return from their hazardous voyages with numerous giant lobsters that had found their way into the nets. Some of them weighed upward of 15 pounds and were usually sold to New York restaurants, but when we had established our connections, I was able to get one now and then.

To cope with an immense lobster requires a utensil of impressive proportions, but I was ready. I had an old copper laundry tub, the oblong kind, which I had had lined with tin. It covered two burners of a large gas stove. The only other requirement was the courage to handle these monsters, to transfer them, while they were thrashing powerfully, from a carton to the boiler—something my husband resolutely refused to have any part of!

On one occasion when I had purchased an especially large and menacing-looking creature, I invited numerous friends to share him with us. The lobster was to be boiled—nothing simpler, nothing more delicious, and contrary to popular belief, not very tough at all. Consequently, a congenial and convivial crowd of sixteen souls was assembled as I exercised all my strength to remove the giant from the great pot.

Everything was in readiness. On the drainboard were a heavy knife and a hammer. Excited, as I always am when I'm approaching something I *know* is going to be splendid tasting, I cut the creature open—and discovered him to be filled with mush. I daresay there's a biological explanation for this condition, but that was hardly in my mind as I considered the difficulty of my immediate position. I had sixteen people to feed and perhaps 3 pounds of solid lobster meat with which to do it.

I confided my perplexity to Donald, who trifled with our guests' appetites by giving them more to drink, while I ransacked my cupboards for anything that would combine happily with lobster—mushrooms, canned tomatoes, rice, saffron, minced clams, olives, and sherry; the type of casserole dish of which I thoroughly disapprove. Yet I found myself with no alternative. My only source of pride lay in the fact that none of our guests left the table hungry.

I've searched my mind for the moral of this story. It seems to be Thurberesque: It's possible to put some trust in an old wives' tale, but not in an old lobster's tail.

Cooking in Liquids

No method of cooking so far described in this book offers so wide a range of dishes to prepare as liquid cooking. Only combination cooking, described in the chapter that follows, is a wealthier source in terms of variety and number. Further (and perhaps more important), none of the processes mentioned hitherto provides so many opportunities to save pennies as does liquid cooking.

There are numerous and satisfying bean dishes which are staple fare in all corners of the world. Conversely, there are some recipes calling for liquid cooking that can devastate your household budget—my own favorite being lobster (God knows, not one that weighs 15 pounds!) boiled in good white wine, an adventure in eating that everyone should enjoy at least once in a lifetime. For simplicity and elegance, it rather resembles that flawless "little black dress" which you can buy off the rack at Bergdorf's for a mere $1,200.

This final chapter on methods of preparing meat, fish, and poultry by "simple" processes deals with the uses of liquids—steaming, boiling, stewing, and poaching—as the means of conveying heat. Most of these techniques involve cooking on the top of the stove, though once you have a stew well under way, you may prefer to place it in your oven. However, it is well to recall that using the oven is generally more fuel-consuming than cooking on a top burner (unless, of course, your stove also serves the purpose of space heater). On the other hand, if for some reason you can't properly regulate a top burner to maintain a simmer temperature, the oven at low heat (250°) is a helpful alternative.

A by-product of most liquid cooking is a sauce or stock. It will not, unfortunately, be so rich as a properly prepared stock of the sort described in the previous chapter. But, all the same, it has its applications.

STEAMING

Steaming is a procedure whereby food is suspended above a boiling liquid and permitted to cook in the vapor. It is not a method that you may employ very often, unless there is some particular dish you are addicted to that happens to call for it; for example, a young roasting chicken or breasts of fowl steamed over a strong, delicious chicken stock. The result gives the bird a flavor incomparably better than that of the more usual boiled chicken, no matter how good or how rich the stock in which you boil it. Steaming is also an excellent technique for preparing fish whose flesh is naturally very firm.

Equipment
For steaming, you need a small metal platform that stands above the liquid in a flat-bottomed pan or pot which can be completely covered. This supports the meat to be steamed, preventing it from being immersed in the water or stock. If you plan to do quite a lot of steaming, you should try to locate a proper steamer. It is usually made of aluminum, with a tight-fitting lid and numerous, fairly wide holes in the bottom. It fits on top of a pot that contains the liquid with which you propose to do the steaming. In addition, you'll require a pancake turner and a pair of tongs.

Techniques of Steaming
Pour your stock or plain water into the pot. Place the steamer on top of it. Into the steamer put the food to be prepared.

Bring the liquid to a boil and allow it to boil briskly until the food is fully cooked.

Steaming isn't a rapid method of cooking. A rough estimate is that it requires about 10 minutes longer per pound than immersion boiling. Among its virtues, however, is that the food is never saturated with moisture, which drains off some of its flavor.

BOILING

This process involves the complete immersion of an ingredient in liquid which is brought to a boil and then made to simmer. To boil meat, you make use of the basic aromatic vegetables and seasonings (carrots, onions, sometimes celery and turnips, parsley, thyme, bay leaf, and occasionally cloves). Depending ultimately on the requirements of the recipe involved, you may need additional vegetables and herbs.

Equipment

A large pot (perhaps your stock pot) of enameled cast iron is much the best—though it is also the most expensive. One wonderful substitute is a big ceramic pot. This, however, you have to "break in," a procedure that takes time. Moreover, it's exceptionally fragile. None is better, though, if you take those two liabilities into account.

You'll need, as well, a sautéing or frying pan, a long wooden spoon for stirring, a large meat fork, a colander, a wide skimmer, and some cheesecloth and string.

Techniques of Boiling

The procedure is similar to the making of stock and calls for the same equipment. Prepare the raw vegetables. Sometimes the recipe calls for sautéing them first. If not, place them in a large pot of cold water.

Bring the water to a boil before introducing the piece of meat. In order to prevent this from disintegrating as it cooks, the meat should be tied into a nice bundle before it is put in the pot. Then bring the water to a boil again.

Skim the surface, and allow the pot to simmer until the meat has been thoroughly cooked.

You'll find that boiled meat can be delicious, especially if you serve it with an appropriately tasty sauce. The cuts of meat which best stand up to this method of cooking are only slightly more expensive than those you buy for making stock.

In boiling, use just enough water to cover the meat and vegetables completely. They should not be allowed to go for a swim! If you plan to serve the boiled meat cold, leave it in the broth to cool.

While it is still slightly tepid, remove it from the liquid, which you should keep, for it becomes a potentially useful by-product in the form of another stock.

Place the meat on a platter, with a second plate or platter on top of it; this should be weighted down heavily to complete the cooling and draining procedure. For this purpose, I make use of the same beautifully rounded stones with which I grind bread crumbs. The pressure exerted on the cooling meat results in a better-shaped and firmer piece; it's easier to slice because it doesn't shred the way a piece does that's still permeated with liquid and unpressed.

Certain boiling recipes demand the cooking of vegetables along with the meat. I beg you not to boil these for hours and hours. It's far preferable to add them to the pot later on in the process, not when you start cooking the meat. At the outset, you should put in only some aromatics such as onions, carrots, etc.—what you choose as flavoring—and don't think of these as vegetables which you'll serve with the meat.

A useful trick is to place the vegetables that will be served in small individual sacks of cheesecloth. This has two advantages: it makes their removal from the pot simpler, and it also facilitates the making of an attractive arrangement of the platter on which you serve the whole finished dish.

Boiled dinners, while fairly quick to prepare, do take quite a long time to cook. They deserve your consideration for a day when you're planning to be home and can thus watch over them. When you're making a boiled dinner, be sure to select a piece of meat that's large enough to provide leftovers—a cold meal or salad or hash of some type.

Foods Suitable for Boiling

BEEF
- Heel of round
- Hind shank
- Rolled plate
- Short ribs
- Brisket
- Corned brisket
- Corned beef
- Rolled neck
- Boneless neck
- Tongue (fresh or corned)

LAMB
- Neck
- Slices
- Riblets
- Shank

VEAL
- Heel of round
- Hind shank
- Breast riblets
- Fore shank

FOWL
- Old chicken
- Young turkey

FISH AND OTHER SEAFOOD
- Large fish (cod, bluefish, bass, haddock)
- Lobster and crayfish
- Crab
- Shrimp and other small crustaceans

VEGETABLES
This is the main way to cook vegetables.

Note: Fish and mollusks should never be boiled except for soups and stews. Fish should be *poached,* and I shall discuss that process later in this chapter.

STEWING

A stew is a boiled preparation in which the vegetables are an essential part of the dish and the fluid is of at least equal importance. Also, the meat included is usually cut into bite-sized pieces, not boiled in a single chunk. The liquor produced by stewing ought to be the best thing about a great stew, and its flavor will be much enhanced by the addition of wine. Thickening of the liquor may be accomplished at the beginning or at the termination of the process.

Stews may be made with meat, fowl, or seafood.

Techniques of Preparing a Meat Stew

Unless you are preparing a particularly elaborate recipe, the steps involved in making a meat stew are genuinely simple.

First, sauté the meat chunks until they are completely browned, so that the juices are sealed within them. The medium for this part of the process may be oil, good drippings, or some melted fat cut from the meat you're about to sauté. When it has been melted, remove the residual particles and then sauté the pieces you wish to brown. You may also use a combination of butter and oil, but in this case it would be a waste, for the more distinctly flavorful fat is better.

After the meat has been browned, you may make a *roux* by adding flour to the melted fat in the sautéing pan, mixing it and browning it. (See Chapter 5, p. 78.) This is added to the stew pot for purposes of thickening the stew. As I noted earlier, you may do this at the end instead of the beginning. If you elect to thicken at the conclusion of the stewing process, you'll use a *beurre manié* (see Chapter 5, p. 80). The advantage of using the French-style *beurre manié* at the end over thickening the stew at the start is that you stand less chance of burning your stew when the juices in which you are cooking are thin; they don't stick to the bottom of the stew pot as much as a thick liquid does.

Add your herbs and spices. Stews can stand a great deal of seasoning, but I urge you to be discreet in your *selection* of these flavorings. Show restraint. Don't empty your spice shelf into the pot; the result can be appalling. It's easy to deceive yourself in this respect—and there is no remedy for it once it's been done. Follow your recipe with care. Otherwise, stick to the introduction of spices whose flavors and intensities you're totally familiar with. (For further counsel, see Chapter 10, devoted to herbs and spices.)

Place the pieces of sautéed meat in the stew pot and cover them with cold water, or with a combination of water and wine—either red or white, though red is more customary with beef.

I start my stew off with a single carrot and a large yellow onion, along with herbs and seasonings to give flavor to the water and wine.

Thereafter, I proceed as I would in the preparation of stock. I normally simmer a stew for about 90 minutes before adding to it the vegetables that are meant for eating.

A stew requires about 3 hours to cook completely. Stews taste better, however, if they're originally prepared 24 hours in advance. Therefore, if you choose to follow this advice, you should cook the stew initially for 30 minutes less than the total time called for in your recipe, then finish the job just before you serve it.

In general, I don't cook my potatoes in the stew pot, but rather steam them separately to preserve their texture and their delicate flavor, then I add them to the stew only when I'm ready to serve it.

To give some variety to your stews, you may substitute other starches for potatoes—noodles, for example.

Cuts of Meat for Stewing

BEEF
  Neck
  Chuck
  Shank
  Flank
  Heel of round
  Cheaper pot roast cuts
  Oxtail

LAMB
  Breast
  Shank
  Neck
  Trotters
  Riblets

VEAL
  Breast
  Shoulder
  Shank
  Heel of round

FOWL AND GAME
  Chicken
  Squab (pigeon)
  Pheasant
  Duck
  Turkey
  Rabbit

We frequently forget that poultry and game form the basis for delicious stews. For these you should use birds that are too tough for other purposes. One of my favorites, an American recipe originally for squirrel, is called Brunswick stew, a genuinely great dish. It can be made with chicken or turkey.

Most cooks stew rabbits, because these creatures tend to dry out when prepared in other ways.

FISH

The preparation of a fish stew involves a procedure slightly different from a meat stew. One important distinction is that it is much more rapid. Also, the recipe may well call for the browning of the vegetables which are to be cooked along with the fish. As soon as the vegetables have been thoroughly cooked, the stew is completed.

A fish stew should be served the day it is prepared. I exhort you to try making this kind of stew. It can be quite incredibly delicious, and it has a peculiar attribute: It is notably less "fishy" than other seafood dishes, because the flavor of the fish is diluted by the liquid in which it has been simmered (to which wine, of course, may be added—dry red or white). This will placate those diners who object to the taste of fish.

For equipment, you require the same kind of pot as is used for making a meat stew. Enameled cast iron is the best. You should *not* use a bare metal utensil for the preparation of fish, because in a matter of minutes the fish will take on a metallic flavor.

Also essential are a sautéing or frying pan, and a long wooden spoon for stirring.

While there is no fish that *isn't* suitable for use in a fish stew, it would be reckless to stew a trout, for instance, or a sole, or a piece of salmon or other premium quality fish. Snapper, pompano, cod, halibut, bass, bluefish, or other fish of good dimensions are good in a stew.

POACHING

To poach is to cook at a barely simmering temperature in the least possible amount of liquid.

There is a particular quality to the process of poaching to which I find it difficult to give verbal expression. Perhaps it has something to do with poaching eggs, which gives them a taste and a texture so different from those of eggs cooked by any other means. The result of poaching is exceptional delicacy of flavor. I'm tempted to settle for the term "fragile." That's almost right, but there's more to it still.

An interesting number and variety of foods, including meat specialties, fowl, and fish, lend themselves to poaching.

Equipment

Poaching is best achieved in a shallow vessel—an oval or circular gratin dish of ceramic, Pyrex, or (my own preference) enameled cast iron. You *can* use an aluminum or iron skillet, but because it may be impregnated with grease or, at the opposite extreme, rust, it really isn't suitable for this kind of liquid cooking. If you acquire a few gratin dishes of different sizes and depths, you'll have the right one for any particular poaching job. As with fish stews, it is wiser not to poach fish in a metal utensil—unless it is enameled.

Patapar and special porous bags may also be used to facilitate the handling of foods poached. Be sure, however, to follow the directions given for their employment.

You should also have two pancake turners (for maneuvering the meat into and out of the poaching utensil), a flame-tamer or trivet (this, especially, if you have difficulty reducing the heat of your burner to a bare simmer), and some paper toweling or cloth for draining.

Techniques of Poaching

Required for proper poaching is just enough liquid—plain water, stock, wine, or a combination of these—to float the piece or pieces of food to be cooked. Into this liquid you place finely chopped or sliced aromatic vegetables and seasonings. The reason for cutting the vegetables in this way is to cause them to give up their flavor to the liquid as quickly as possible.

Boil the liquid for 20 minutes. Then, with infinite care, introduce the food to be poached and immediately reduce the heat to the lowest simmer.

Cook for about 20 minutes, or perhaps a little longer, until the food is just cooked.

Gently remove the food and place it on a paper towel or a piece of linen to drain and dry.

That's really all there is to it!

(The poaching of eggs is discussed in Chapter 7, given over exclusively to the egg.)

Foods Suitable for Poaching

MEATS

Meats as such can't be satisfactorily poached. However, some meat by-products—like brains and sweetbreads—are especially delicious when poached.

FOWL

The breast of any fowl is preferred, but other parts may also be poached.

FISH

All kinds of fish, whole and fillets.

5

Modifiers: *Preparations for Combination and Sauce Cookery*

Getting Ready for College

Not all of the techniques elucidated in this chapter are directly related to each other. They are processes you must understand, however, before you involve yourself with combination cooking and saucemaking. These are both primary and final steps that take cooking from the ordinary to the sublime, that make for truly sophisticated work. None requires a great deal of time. The rewards are disproportionately large for the minutes you devote to them.

There are several procedures that must be elucidated before I come to the essence of this grammar of cooking: combination cooking, or the construction of the compound sentence.

Preparations for Combination Cookery
LARDING

Larding is the insertion of pieces of fat into the flesh of lean meat. The fat is either salt pork or pork fatback cut into thin strips.

The reason for larding a chunk of lean meat is to increase the amount of fat and therefore the flavor and the moisture which the fat provides. Since larding does add moisture, it makes the meat juicier, and helps to reduce shrinkage in the cooking process.

I wrote earlier in these pages about barding, the wrapping of fat around a piece of lean meat. Barding is quite often (but mistakenly) treated as a synonym for larding. I can't think why this should be so, for there is no similarity of procedure.

Pot roasts and other large pieces of lean meat such as chuck for dishes other than roasts should be larded. You may also lard a whole filet of beef or a whole liver when braising it.

Equipment
A small knife or a special larding needle.

Techniques of Larding
With a small sharp knife (or, better still, with a special larding needle—a long, hollow, pointed tube), you insert the strips of fat every 3 inches, usually *across* the grain of the meat. Your recipe will advise you whether to lard with the grain of the meat or across it.

If you wish to add extra flavor, you may marinate the strips of fat before using them for larding purposes.

MARINATING

A marinade is a liquid or a blending of salt and spices that you use to saturate, impregnate, and, at the same time, tenderize a piece of meat. A marinade may be used in any form of cooking, but it is generally reserved for combination procedures, since it works so effectively on the tougher cuts of meat normally employed in them. However, I *always* marinate pork for roasting, because I like the flavor the marinade conveys. Legs of lamb also lend themselves to marinating. Chuck, rump, shoulder, breast, flank, hocks are all improved by this procedure.

A *liquid* marinade is composed of wine (red or white) or vinegar, oil, salt, pepper, spices, and often aromatic vegetables. All good cookbooks furnish you with at least one recipe for marinade. Try them out until you discover one that provides the taste you prefer. My own favorites are found in the first volume of *Mastering the Art of French Cooking*.

A *dry* marinade consists of salt and spices which you rub into the surface of the meat.

The remainder of the marinating technique is the same for dry and liquid forms.

Equipment

A covered container, ceramic or enameled metal, just large enough to allow you to cover the meat completely with a liquid marinade.

In the case of a *dry* marinade, a bowl or container with a cover; again, just of sufficient size to contain the cut being treated. A cake platter may be substituted.

Techniques of Marinating

Enclose the meat and the marinade in a cooking pot which is just large enough to contain the cut of meat. The container should *not* be of metal (unless enameled), but must have a tight cover in order to permit the meat to absorb the aromas of the marinade for a minimum of 8 hours, preferably for 24 hours. There are occasions when you may want to extend the marinating for two or three days.

MIREPOIX

A *mirepoix* is a bed of vegetables. In fact, it is made up of those aromatic vegetables—carrots, onions, bay leaves, parsley, thyme (and, now and then, garlic and/or celery)—that are used in the making of stocks and stews. A *mirepoix* may be used with a roast, if you are seeking a more subtle or complicated flavor than the one obtainable by simple roasting of the meat. A *mirepoix* has a dramatic effect as well on the sauce in which you finally serve the roast.

Equipment
A frying pan or sautéing pan.

A knife for cutting up the aromatic vegetables, herbs, and spices.

A wooden spoon.

A vegetable peeler.

A large jar (if you plan to make more *mirepoix* than is required for the task immediately at hand).

Techniques of Preparing a Mirepoix
Even if the recipe you are following doesn't specifically call for it, you should consider sautéing the *mirepoix* before use. For this purpose you can use butter, oil, bacon fat, or the wonderful fat you have skimmed from the top of your stock (if you've thought to start saving that). This is an ideal use for that fat or some other special fat you've accumulated.

The *mirepoix* should be sautéed for 8 to 10 minutes, until the vegetables are soft and begin to sweat—that is, give off their juices. The reasons for sautéing a *mirepoix* are to retard its tendency to burn during the subsequent cooking processes and to release its flavor.

Be certain that you lay your meat, fowl, or fish on a bed of *mirepoix* that is thick enough to cover the entire bottom of the cooking utensil.

If the heat of your kitchen isn't too great (i.e., if it's not summertime), the meat will better take on the wonderful attributes of the marinade if left out of the refrigerator. In any case, you'll have to bring it up to room temperature before you start to cook it.

If you're marinating with a liquid, you must turn the meat occasionally so that all its surfaces are equally exposed to the marinade. Wipe the meat with a paper towel to dry it before starting to cook it. The residue of marinade in the soaking pot will often be added to the liquor in which the meat is to be prepared.

BLANCHING

Blanching is the application of hot water for the purpose of cleansing and/or loosening the outer covering of certain cuts of meat, particularly specialties like heads, feet, brains, sweetbreads, shanks, kidneys, etc., and for the removal of excess salt. It is not a complete cooking method, but rather a preliminary for combination cooking.

Pieces are first soaked for a time in cold water which should be changed once to remove the blood that has drained off.

When completely cleaned, they are placed in a pan containing lots of cold water and brought to a boil.

Feet and heads should be boiled for 20 minutes.

Veal sweetbreads need 10 minutes of boiling. Lamb sweetbreads and all varieties of brains need only to be brought to a boil.

You need only blanch such foods if you are planning to cut them up, sauté them, braise them, and serve them with a sauce.

It is not necessary to blanch if you're using these kinds of foods in a stew-type dish, for the normal routine of starting them off in cold water, bringing them to a boil, and skimming the surface will adequately purify them—which is, as I remarked, the reason for blanching.

When you are making a *mirepoix* (and if you have the time), it is worthwhile to sauté a surplus of it which you can store in a jar in your refrigerator.

MATIGNON

Matignon is the rich cousin of the *mirepoix*. It consists of the same herbs and chopped vegetables, but blanched salt pork, ham, or bacon is added to this combination (chopping is easier if you slice your vegetables first). Other ingredients are tomatoes and green peppers (or, for a more forceful taste, Italian or bell peppers). I always use a *matignon* as a base when I'm preparing fish.

Techniques of Preparing a Matignon

The procedure is similar to that of *mirepoix,* except that you chop the vegetables, adding shallots, ham, blanched salt pork, or bacon. When I am using the *matignon* with fish, I put in seeded tomatoes.

When you've finished sautéing the *matignon,* stir in some Madeira. You should invest in a bottle of this delicious fortified wine exclusively for cooking. Don't let anyone drink it up, for nothing can stimulate the flavor of a dish so simply as the addition of a few splashes of Madeira. It is also a wonderful additive for easy sauces.

These preliminaries may seem pointless, until you've begun to sauté your first batch of *matignon.* A single whiff of the aroma will help to explain their purpose. Following these procedures is by way of going the extra mile which will make a good dish sublime. For the dedicated cook, nothing could be more worthwhile.

Preparations for Saucemaking

Roux is the French word for the fat and flour beginning of a cream sauce. As described below, there are three kinds of *roux*. Basically, all are similar to the American technique, except that we don't always make the distinctions noted here.

Both *roux* and *beurre manié* are French methods to thicken a cream sauce. *Beurre manié* is infinitely superior to the American way of making a flour and water paste to give final body to a sauce. And *roux* offers much greater scope in the starting of sauces as well.

For both processes, you mix flour with fat. Flour blends very well with hot fat. The particles of flour distribute themselves evenly throughout the heated grease and afford you much less hazard of lumpiness when the proportions are correct and the mixture is stirred vigorously. Never guess about the proportions or you'll be courting disaster. If you've made too little for your purposes of thickening, you can easily and quickly make more. If you find that you've prepared too much, you can save it in your refrigerator.

ROUX

For starting a sauce or a thick soup, you should first make a *roux*. There are three types: brown, pale, and white. The sort of *roux* you select will depend on the kind of liquid you're going to use it with.

White *roux* is for use with milk, cream, fish, or chicken stock.

Pale *roux* is for blending with veal stock.

Brown *roux* is used in combination with a brown stock or for making a brown sauce.

The three varieties of *roux* are different from each other only in that they are cooked for different lengths of time. White *roux* is heated just to the point when the flour begins to scorch. The flour of pale *roux* is just slightly scorched. It is more deeply scorched when brown *roux* is desired. In all three cases, however, the flour must be thoroughly cooked. This only presents a possible problem in the case of white *roux*. It should be cooked just to the point when the flour and the fat have combined completely, then heated gently over a flame-tamer until the flour is no longer raw to the taste.

In general, the fat employed for the making of white *roux* should be butter. For pale or brown *roux*, you may use other fats, such as the skimmings from stock. Let your palate and purpose be your guides.

Equipment

You need a saucepan with a thick bottom, or a small skillet, for the making of *roux*. If you are afraid you may scorch the white *roux*, use a double boiler. But it is simpler to employ a single utensil, if possible. I use a double boiler to make white *roux* only when I want to hold a white sauce —i.e., keep it for a while before using it. A flame-tamer is very handy and with care it can take the place of a double boiler.

You will also need a wire whisk, a slotted wooden spoon, or a wooden paddle with a hole in the center of it. You may also stir with a Swedish whisk, which is made of a bunch of small wooden sticks wired together at the handle end.

Techniques of Preparing a Roux

Using equal parts, melt butter or fat in the pan, then stir in flour.

All forms of *roux* should be prepared over a low heat. If overcooked and consequently burned, the flour will lose its capacity to thicken. When making *roux*, stir the combination constantly.

Pale and brown *roux* are cooked in identical ways, save only that the former requires less time. The mixture will give off a slightly nutty odor as it is cooking.

The three kinds may be prepared ahead of time and set aside, if this is more convenient. Then, just before using, you need only rewarm them in order to combine them with the hot stock or other liquid.

The general rule for proper quality is equal parts of flour and fat.

The great Escoffier calls for 8 parts of fat to 9 parts of flour, which begins to involve one in higher mathematics. As a rough guide, 50–50 is sufficiently reliable.

Roux may be safely stored in tightly sealed jars in the refrigerator for a couple of weeks.

BEURRE MANIÉ

Beurre manié is 1 part flour and 2 parts fat, usually butter, kneaded together to form a dough ball. It is used when you require a little thickening for a sauce or a stew or a fish dish and is added at the end of the cooking process. *Beurre manié* may also come to your rescue if the sauce you have made with a *roux* isn't sufficiently thick.

Techniques of Preparing Beurre Manié

Knead (with your fingers, as already noted) 2 parts of butter to 1 part of flour and drop the resulting lump into the liquid you want to thicken, stirring thoroughly. Allow the mixture to cook for some minutes in order to achieve the thickening desired, being sure that the flour is completely cooked before serving the dish.

Starches other than flour may be used—cornstarch, rice or potato flour, for example. For most Chinese cooking, employ cornstarch. However, you will normally use half as much cornstarch as flour. Always add cornstarch to a cold liquid, and *never* apply a high heat to this preparation. Cornstarch should be added directly to the liquid that needs thickening, and not be mixed with fat. The other substitutes, rice and potato flour, are used in the same proportion as cornstarch. They are, however, to be mixed with fat. High heat should be avoided.

The deployment of these other starches appreciably changes the texture of a sauce. For instance, I prefer a potato flour to thicken cream soups. Cornstarch makes a sauce translucent.

6

The Compound Sentence:
Combination Cooking

The Sauce Wasn't Really the Gravy!

An aunt of mine visited us quite frequently when I was a child. According to the family account, she had been a "real beauty" in her youth. Her heart "had been broken" when her fiancé had died during the influenza epidemic of 1917. She had never married. It sometimes seemed to me that the greatest pleasure she derived from visiting us was to patronize my mother and to imply that every aspect of our household would be far better managed if *she* were in charge of it. She was a mine of volunteered information; this ran from places where Mother could buy the best hall carpeting at reasonable prices to the size of potato that was the most prudent purchase. One wondered how our home functioned at all without her in her merciful periods of absence.

Once while this aunt was on a visit to our house, Mother dismissed a cook who had been in her employ for many years. Perhaps, after a lapse of so long a time, I read too much into the incident now, in which I perceive the work of her maidenly hand. Mother was the one who interviewed candidates for a replacement, and Mother made the final selection herself—though the aunt offered a lot of coaching. She quoted their mother, my maternal grandmother, a figure revered even more in death than in life: "Mother always said that when you hire a new cook you should have her make a pot roast. A good gravy is the surest test of a good cook."

It may well be that my intense dislike for the word "gravy" dates from that episode. The term has always held for me the vision (and how my own children enjoy teasing me by referring to "gravy"!) of a lumpy, gray sauce, too thick, filled with commercial additives, and endowed with a taste that has little or no relation to the flavor of the roast whose by-product it is supposed to be. The word "gravy" will not appear again in these pages. I shall discuss "juices" and "sauces."

No matter how annoying it so frequently was, my aunt's counsel wasn't invariably bad. Of course, no cook can demonstrate a comprehensive culinary mastery by the preparation of a single dish, no matter how superior it proves. On the other hand, the creation of a pot roast, which is the product of combination cooking, demonstrates much more of one's talents than the fabrication of a meal consisting of a roast, vegetables, and potatoes.

What Is Combination Cooking?

Combination cooking is the harmonizing of two or more of the basic routines of cookery. The different kinds of combination cooking are:

Braising
Pot roasting

Fricasseeing
À la poêle (a French style of covered-pan frying)
En casserole and en cocotte
Au gratin
Glazing

In other words, combination cooking is a series of blendings, like chemical formulas, of methods of preparation earlier described. When using them in conjunction with each other, American cookbook writers lump the combining of cooking processes under the general (and generally misleading) heading of "casserole cooking."

If you have been reading this volume in the order in which it was put together, you will have already covered the elements involved in combination cooking. This chapter is intended to help you understand just how these various procedures may be allied, sometimes with a change of ingredients, to produce nearly all the rest of the main dishes that are referred to, confusingly, as entrées.

Nothing in all of cooking gives me a feeling of greater satisfaction and of time well spent than the confection of certain combination dishes—not even the baking of a perfect cake or the creation of a perfect sauce or soup, and soup is my favorite food. The perfumes, the bastings, the sights of these productions in process, the sense of involvement, are all sources of enormous pleasure to me.

If you peruse any cookbook (save those which offer recipes that call for canned soups as a panacea), you will receive at least *some* hints of the delights that lie in store for you. For combination cooking is the method that demands of you the actual construction of a dish!

You may prefer to be traditional, electing to follow a given recipe to the letter, as I often do myself. At other times, however, I combine my own choice of ingredients, though staying within the rules that govern the general procedure called for, which is basically braising. Even if you are creating your own dish, I urge you most strongly to be scrupulous in adhering to these rules—for in these directions lies certainty of success.

BRAISING

Braising involves the deployment of the following procedures which we have already covered:

- You may blanch your meat.
- You may marinate it.
- You may lard it, if it's lean, or bard it, if this is required.
- You will sauté the meat.
- You will make use of a *mirepoix* or a *matignon*.
- And, finally, you will use your stock or wine to stew the meat—that is, to braise it.

Before discussing the steps involved in braising and before offering explanations of this process, I want to give some space to a discussion of the kinds of meat that are suitable for the purpose.

A cardinal rule is not to use a piece for braising that is either too small or too thin.

You can braise any sort of meat, but it would be rather extravagant to employ a piece of first quality meat such as a filet or a rib roast. In the first place, such a cut would disintegrate. In the second, braising destroys the natural flavor of these pieces, so why spoil them?

What is great about braising is the effect it has on a large chunk of meat which, under ordinary cooking techniques like roasting, would be so tough as to be inedible. You can transform it into a dish that is unusual—much less monotonous and much more interesting than a regular steak or roast.

Don't forget to order more meat than will be required for the original meal, for the leftovers from braising are delicious.

Perhaps it is a matter of purely personal judgment, but I don't have the same misgivings about using a leg of lamb for braising that I have about the finer cuts of beef. I find the change of flavor a boon—occasionally, at any rate.

As I've indicated in an earlier chapter, you can roast a breast of veal, lamb, or pork, but all are infinitely better if you braise them—suitable for presentation to the most special of your guests.

This matter of personal taste is, of course, terribly important. For instance, due to the prejudices of my husband and sons, I'm only allowed to serve ham in my house if I braise it in white wine. Many people are of the identical opinion once they have savored ham prepared in this way —permeated with the flavor of the wine, stock, vegetables, and herbs.

You'll observe from the list that follows that braising fundamentally calls for second-cut meats and turns them into first-class food.

Braising is also excellent for game, like venison. There are some cooks who will only prepare game in this way.

Cuts of Meat for Braising

BEEF
- Heel of round
- Hind shank
- Flank
- Flank steak
- Plate
- Short ribs
- Brisket
- Crosscut
- English-cut arm pot roast
- Arm steak
- Rump
- Pot roast
- Chuck pot roast
- Shoulder filet
- Neck
- Tongue
- Sweetbreads
- Liver

LAMB
- Leg
- Blade chops
- Square-cut shoulder
- Rolled shoulder
- Neck slices
- Riblets
- Breast
- Shank
- Tongue
- Kidney
- Sweetbreads
- Liver

VEAL
- Rump
- Kidney
- Loin
- Sirloin
- Rib chop
- Rib roast
- Arm roast
- Blade roast
- Arm steak
- Blade steak
- Shoulder roast
- Heel of round
- Hind shank
- Scallops of veal
- Breast riblets
- Foreshank
- Tongue
- Sweetbreads

PORK
- Tenderloin
- Chops
- Blade
- Ham
- Spare ribs
- Hock
- Arm steak
- Kidneys
- Liver

FOWL AND GAME
- Turkey
- Duck
- Squab
- Game birds
- Livers of all fowl
- Venison, etc.

Equipment
- Sautéing or frying pan
- Large pot with a tightly fitting lid
- Strainer
- Baster
- Wooden spoon

You need a heavy pot which can be placed in the oven, preferably one of the enameled, cast-iron utensils I've mentioned so often, a Dutch oven, or any other substantial pot of metal or earthenware. Its size is important. It must *just* contain the meat, without permitting the lid to press down on it. If you braise in a pot that is too large for the job, you'll be wildly extravagant. It is far better (and cheaper in the long run) to invest in just the right size of pot than constantly to have to purchase extra quantities of wine and make large amounts of stock and vegetables to fill a container that is too large for the piece of meat you're braising.

Techniques of Braising
There are two basic methods of braising; the one you select depends on the kind of meat you're planning to serve.

The first is for use with red meats such as beef, real mutton, or game—heavy, tough pieces of meat.

The second is for "white" meats such as ham, pork, veal, tongue, lamb, fowl, and sweetbreads. This process is somewhat closer to a roasting technique.

You should first marinate beef, mutton, and game.

It is not necessary to marinate other cuts, except pork, but I recommend it all the same. When in doubt, let the recipe you've selected be your guide.

Always marinate your meat for at least 8 hours—24 hours if possible.

If the meat is lean, lard it.

Sauté the meat in order to sear it.

If you have had it in a marinade, first dry it with paper towels before sautéing it.

If the meat to be braised is one of the tougher cuts, you should initially sauté it to a brown that is much darker than for cuts that are more tender.

If the piece you are braising seems not lean enough to require larding, but is nevertheless not very fatty, you may want to bard it after you've completed the sautéing.

The reason for sautéing as the first step is identical to the explanation for it offered earlier: It seals in the juices, making it possible for them to travel inward during the initial stage of cooking as they do in roasting, working their way toward the center of the cut.

If you *have not* marinated the meat, you'll have to make a *mirepoix*. If you've used a marinade, you should take the vegetables from that preparation and use them instead of a *mirepoix*. You may find that you'll have to increase the quantity somewhat.

Remember to cook the vegetables (if you're employing those salvaged from the marinade) until they sweat, i.e., until they are soft and giving off their juices, using the good fat which you've skimmed from the surface of your stock. This not only provides a better flavor for the vegetables, as I've observed, but also prevents them from burning.

The *mirepoix* or *matignon* is placed in the bottom of the pot, forming a bed on which the meat will be braised. If a marinade has been used, pour the drained-off liquid over the meat and put the lid on the pot.

Using a high heat on top of the stove, boil the pot until the marinade becomes syrupy. Then add stock—a brown stock for beef, some chicken dishes, and tongue; you may also use a *pot au feu* stock. The use of a chicken or veal stock should be confined to dishes of chicken or veal. Add enough stock to cover the meat.

When braising more tender cuts, you may employ a mixture consisting half of veal stock, half of red or white wine, according to your own taste and/or the requirements of the recipe you're following.

BRAISING RED MEATS

It is at this point that the two braising methods diverge. First I shall describe the technique for beef, mutton, and game. You place the pot directly into a moderate (350°) oven, on the middle shelf. It should cook quietly for 90 to 120 minutes.

Near the end of this period, prick the surface of the meat to see if the juices are running clear. When they are, it means that the blood has decomposed and that the essences have drained to the center of the cut. The initial phase of the braising process is completed at that point.

By now the pot liquors are no longer covering the meat. At this juncture, you must turn the piece over and begin to baste it. This is of vital importance. If you don't baste the meat from now on, it will dry out.

The second phase of this braising process begins when the juices have all collected at the center of the cut, where they immediately begin to evaporate. Once this point has been reached, the laws of physics being what they are, the vapors move back toward the surface, causing the tough fibers to break down and, thus, tenderizing the meat as they travel.

On reaching the surface of the meat, the juices flow out again and mix with the pot liquors. Then (because you're constantly basting) these fluids re-enter the meat, giving it the special flavor that is unique to the braised dish, whether you serve it hot or cold.

The cooking is completed when you can insert a dull knife or a cooking spoon easily all the way to the center of the cut—proof indeed that it is tender to the heart.

Total cooking time is about 4 hours. If a longer period is required, there need be no problem. You can't overcook by the braising process—except, of course, by allowing it to burn or dry out. However, since you've been basting it religiously, this can't occur. You may, however, find it necessary to add more liquid—wine and/or stock—if the original liquors have vanished.

BRAISING "WHITE" MEATS

The braising of "white" meats involves a method different from the point indicated above—after the first stages of preparation. Remember, though, that you don't sauté white meats to so dark a shade of brown as the heavier cuts.

Place the "white" meat on its bed of vegetables.

Pour into the pot a couple of inches of veal stock. Put on the lid and place the pot on the top of the stove, cooking it at high heat until the stock has been reduced to a syrupy consistency. Baste the meat lavishly and often.

Turn the piece over and repeat the process, adding more stock for the purpose, so as to make enough of the gelatinous substance inherent in veal broth to coat the meat well before cooking it in the oven. This will help to make it more tender.

Add an amount of wine equal to the quantity of reduced stock and bring it to a boil.

Set the pot in a moderate (350°) oven, placing it on the middle shelf.

Be sure to baste it frequently. Otherwise, the meat will dry out very quickly.

The process is completed when you prick the meat and find that the juice runs clear. The time involved is about the same as for standard oven roasting of the same kind of cut.

A cautionary note about veal: It can be overcooked, in which event it will simply disintegrate into fibers.

BRAISING SWEETBREADS

The procedure for braising sweetbreads is the same as for "white" meats, except that they require only about 45 minutes in the oven. Blanching is the first step in making sweetbreads, after which you bring them to a boil and then simmer or cook in the oven.

BRAISING TONGUE

This is similar to the preparation of sweetbreads. Be guided by a good cookbook. Tongue takes a good long time to cook.

BRAISING KIDNEYS

Strictly speaking, you can't braise kidneys because the process would destroy them. There are, however, two related methods of preparing them (apart from broiling). One is to blanch them and then stew them. The other requires that they first be sautéed in oil and butter very rapidly, while being stirred constantly for 3 or 4 minutes. Then they are placed in a colander and allowed to drain for at least 10 minutes, while you prepare a wine or Madeira sauce, in which you simply heat them through. The result is succulent and tender kidneys.

The Use of Bones in Braising

When you are studying recipes for braising, you may see that the deployment of bones is called for and you may, as a result, wonder why I have failed to make mention of them until now. *The* master, Escoffier, felt that braising doesn't require enough time to make the use of bones worthwhile, because to retrieve their essence demands the lapse of 3 hours or more. A second objection to the use of bones is that it requires a much larger pot, consequently the introduction of much more liquid, which will not be reduced so rapidly and thus not produce so delicious a result. I must note in passing, however, that despite my near idolatry of Maître Escoffier, I make use of calves' feet or pigs' feet if I plan to serve a braised dish cold, for both are filled with the glutinous matter that makes gelatin.

Some Thoughts About Braising Recipes

When I'm following a braising recipe for the very first time, I always follow it closely. No matter how practiced a cook you are, you can't come to a firm conclusion about it from "tasting" as you read—though in most other instances fine cooks can judge, from a perusal of a recipe, just what the resulting dish will taste like, just as a fine musician can "hear" a score by simply reading it.

In the case of combination cooking, however, this is not the case. You must actually taste and chew the product in order to be certain.

What I've attempted here is an explanation of the braising process, as completely as I can make it, with all the steps required.

This is not a recipe. For recipes, I urge you again to consult some of the cookbooks you admire, or to see the bibliography at the end of this book. There you'll find directions somewhat less exhaustive than those provided here. Assuming that you understand the *nature* of the process, no recipe should give you any trouble. The amounts of time required depend, as remarked, on the type of meat to be braised.

There *is* one final point: Please sauté the vegetables, whether the recipe you are following calls for this or not.

POT ROASTING

Pot roast and *sauerbraten* are simply cousins of braising. My personal conviction is that once you have tried your hand at braising and discovered its range of possibilities and flavors, you'll return to it often.

Recipes for pot roast and *sauerbraten* seldom mention the need for larding or barding. According to the meat you use, I would recommend following one of those procedures anyhow. Though one of our great cooks declares the processes no longer necessary because the quality of our meats is now so good, I'm sure his privileged position with butchers leads him to this deceptive conclusion. He just doesn't have to deal with run-of-the-market meat, which is all that the rest of us usually find available.

Cuts of Meat for Pot Roasting
The same meats are suitable for these processes as for braising (see pp. 85–86).

Equipment
The pot to employ is the same kind used for braising, i.e., earthenware, a Dutch oven, or an enameled cast-iron utensil with a tightly fitting lid.

Techniques of Pot Roasting
Roll the meat in flour which has been flavored with salt, pepper, and other spices.

Sauté it in fat.

Cook it in plain water for the same period required for braising a piece of meat of similar size and toughness.

FRICASSEEING

To fricassee is to follow a procedure that is similar to braising, except that the meat you prepare is always cut up into small chunks—1½ inches for meats and individual joints for fowl (the breast may be cut into two pieces).

Cuts of Meat for Fricasseeing
Fricassee can be made with beef, lamb, veal, chicken, and rabbit.

For fricassee, you would use any of the cuts suitable for braising, especially those containing bone. It would not be worthwhile to use the big "roast" sort of piece, since you have to cut it up.

Techniques of Fricasseeing

Generally, the meat and vegetables are initially browned. Note that the vegetables are not prepared in the form of a *mirepoix*, rather, they are cut into larger pieces, as for a stew.

In a pot like the one used for braising or pot roasting, the meat is cooked slowly in the oven or on top of the stove.

Toward the end of the process, a rich, thick sauce is made and poured over the meat, enough having been prepared to render the final dish very like a stew.

Total cooking time is about 2 hours.

À LA POÊLE

There is no one English word that translates the French *poêle*. The word can mean both stove and cooking pot, and as a method of cooking, it is not one that we use in the United States. It is braising in fat, usually butter, the same cuts of meat used in braising.

I've already mentioned that braising is a fundamental part of what we describe as "casserole cooking." Cooking *à la poêle* is its spendthrift cousin! The principal differences between the two are the use of fat and the absence of liquid in cooking *à la poêle* until the very end of the process, when wine and/or stock may be added.

Techniques of Preparing à la Poêle

Making use of the large, tight-lidded Dutch oven or casserole, place a layer of *uncooked matignon* at the bottom of the pot. On top of this bed of vegetables, place a piece of tender meat, well seasoned.

Melt some butter and pour a generous quantity over the meat.

Cover the pan and place it in a moderate (350°) oven, on the middle shelf.

Baste from time to time, adding more melted butter whenever necessary. (If you're very careful, you can use margarine, but beware the problem of too high a temperature. Margarine is certainly less expensive, but I prefer to find other ways of economizing.)

When the meat is cooked (as soon as the juice is running clear), uncover it and allow it to brown in the oven, raising the temperature to 450°. The cooking time is difficult to estimate. It will depend entirely on the size and/or the relative toughness of the meat.

As soon as the meat has been sufficiently browned, remove the pot from the oven and set the meat aside. Pour some heated stock into the pot, stirring it into the vegetables at the bottom. Bring this mixture to a boil on top of the stove and allow it to boil gently for 10 minutes.

Strain off the vegetables, clearing the liquid of some of its fat as well. A good way to do this is by using a syringe-type baster. (Don't forget to save the fat to use in other cooking, as you use fats salvaged from stockmaking.)

When cooking game birds *à la poêle*, add burned brandy —heat brandy in small pan and light—for the final 10 minutes of cooking.

You may also stuff birds or meats for preparation by this method, but if you do, remember to allow almost double the cooking time.

EN CASSEROLE AND *EN COCOTTE*

These are variations of cooking *à la poêle*. Indeed, it is mainly a question of nomenclature. *En casserole* would describe an unstuffed bird or a piece of meat that has been prepared in a casserole.

En cocotte is actually a description of a process that occurs during the final 20 minutes of preparing a dish *à la poêle.* At this point, you add whatever vegetables you wish to serve with the meat, after having previously sautéed them until they are almost completely cooked. Cover the pot and finish the cooking of meat and vegetables together.

The usual recipe calls for removing the meat and vegetables in order to make the accompanying sauce with heated stock. Though my own variation is somewhat unorthodox, it works: I put them back into the pot in which they were cooked and serve them directly from that container.

AU GRATIN

This is a process of heating food which has been previously cooked (occasionally it is raw, however), with a covering of thick sauce, usually flavored with cheese and sprinkled with bread crumbs and butter or sometimes with grated cheese. You may cook *au gratin* in either your oven or broiler. When a brown crust forms on the surface of the sauce, it is ready to serve.

GLAZING

Glazing is a final step in the preparation of a dish, hot or cold, from main course to dessert, whenever you want it covered with a smooth, glossy finish.

You may glaze with butter, thick sauces, cheese, *glace de viande,* meat juices, gelatin, honey, sugar syrups, jellies, liquefied jams, and chocolate.

Techniques of Glazing
BUTTER GLAZING

Pour lots of melted butter over the dish to be glazed. Place it in a hot broiler to brown. If you do your butter glazing in an oven, place the dish in a pan of cold water so as to prevent overcooking the already cooked food.

THICK-SAUCE GLAZING
Coat the food with either a béchamel or Mornay sauce. Dust the surface with grated cheese, then brown it under a hot broiler.

MEAT GLAZING
This is done by placing a braised or roast cut of meat in the oven after having coated its surface with juices which have been greatly reduced.

GLAZING WITH JELLY, HONEY, OR SYRUP
Meats like ham or tongue are coated with a mixture of mustard and jelly, honey, or syrup. Then the meat is placed in a 325°–350° oven to brown and glaze.

GLAZING COLD DESSERTS
Make a glaze of honey, jelly, or syrup. Heat any of these preparations until they liquefy. Then brush them over the surfaces of cakes, pies, or tarts.

GLAZING WITH SUGAR
Sprinkle cooked vegetables with brown or white sugar. Place them in a hot oven and cook until the sugar coating melts, browns, and becomes glazed.

A similar effect can be obtained on cakes and other desserts with sugar (brown or white). The glazing is accomplished, however, in a medium broiler which you can watch with care, removing the dish as soon as the browning and glazing have been achieved.

FORCEMEATS: MEAT LOAF, *PÂTÉ*, AND SAUSAGE

Forcemeats, sausages, and meat loaves are *not* combination cooking, but rather a combination of ingredients thoroughly blended, and baked or boiled.

Forcemeats: Meat Loaf, Pâté, and Sausage

It may appear odd that I should write of such apparently different subjects as meat loaf, *pâté,* and sausage in the same section. However, they are cousins—all forcemeats, that is, chopped or minced meats.

That almost universal favorite, meat loaf, has the advantage of being a relatively inexpensive dish to prepare, inasmuch as one can introduce bread crumbs and, in the recipe I follow, milk as well, to stretch the meat. The best meat loaf is made with equal parts of beef, veal, and pork, and it is invariably baked.

Nothing enhances one's reputation as a fine cook so readily as the creation of a *pâté*—or one of *its* cousins, *terrine, galantine, ballottine,* or *pâté en croûte.* Some of these preparations contain liver, many contain large portions of fat, and the quantities of different chopped meats vary from one to another, as do the herbs, spices, wines, and brandy employed. Nevertheless, the various *pâtés* are really just exotic meat loaves. You need have no great apprehensions about preparing them if you have a good mincer or a heavy-duty blender. The addition of nuts, chicken breasts, ham, or even truffles adds to the flavor and certainly increases the awe of the people served, but it does not add significantly to the complication of preparation—anymore than does the spreading of layers of cheese in a macaroni casserole.

The word *pâté,* which I shall continue to use, is actually a misnomer for all but the *pâté en croûte* or other dishes of this nature enclosed in a crust. The misuse occurs in French as well as English. What is meant is really forcemeat. *Pâté en croûte* is a forcemeat with a crust baked in a mold. *Terrine* is baked in an earthenware or porcelain crock.

Ballottine is another misnomer, for any rolled roast (in France) is a *ballottine,* not merely a hot forcemeat with a cylindrical shape. The proper term is *galantine,* which is a forcemeat wrapped securely in cloth and cooked in stock.

I became a sausage-maker when we were living in Ireland. My family wanted Italian-American and American-style sausage, finding the native varieties of "bangers" too bland. All sausages are forcemeats, varying in proportion of lean to fat meat from 1 to 1 to 1 to 2. The basic ingredient, of course, is pork, though some sausage recipes call for the addition of beef or lamb. I used to grind up equal parts of lean and fat pork which, by the kind of spices I added, I could turn into American- or Italian-style sausages. They are generally panfried or baked. I usually start sausage off in boiling water, then finish the cooking in a frying pan.

Salami, bologna, and similar preparations are simply forcemeats which have been smoked or cured and dried.

7

The Pluperfect: *The Egg and Its Special Dishes*

The Indispensable Egg

Leonardo da Vinci, the greatest of all Renaissance figures, described the egg as having the perfect form. Whatever one feels aesthetically about it, the role of the egg in cooking is unique. In spite of the tarnish attached to its reputation by some because of its tendency to generate cholesterol, it is still nearly the perfect food.

In most instances, you really don't have to worry about the use of eggs, because the individual portion of the yolk that you consume is very small. Moreover, penny for penny, nothing affords greater nourishment than the egg.

An understanding of the egg in cooking is essential to the rest of this book.

The egg can be prepared in a myriad of ways in dishes in which it is the central feature. Consider its function in the making of some soups, sauces, cakes, soufflés, custards, mousses, and other dishes, none of which would be possible without the egg.

There has to be great interest, in these days of high meat prices, in the soufflés and mousses which can be substituted for dishes requiring meat. Another point in favor of these two types of recipes is that they are much less fattening than pastas and other starchy preparations. And although they do demand real attention, they don't take very long to make.

Many desserts and all cakes depend on eggs. The same may be said about the entire family of custards, including the *quiche*, which is becoming increasingly popular. Many sauces—notably those perennial favorites, hollandaise and mayonnaise—couldn't be made without eggs. And eggs are required for the thickening of many other kinds of sauces and soups.

When I was on a diet some years ago, I wanted to prepare a sauce that would make a piece of fish taste like a product of *haute cuisine*, not a bland dieter's fare. From some mushroom peels and stems, which I boiled for 30 minutes, I made an essence, using an egg yolk as the thickening agent. Not only did the resulting mixture taste rich, but it was endowed with a dense, unctuous texture—something normally unexpected in a low-calorie meal.

I strongly recommend that you consult your favorite cookbook and familiarize yourself with the wealth of egg dishes that are available, many of them quick to prepare, simple, and inexpensive.

MASTERING THE EGG

The egg has a temperament which can be rather alarming, and mastery of it can be achieved only by experience.

The first thing to bear in mind is that the best egg is a fresh egg—something best recalled by the pejorative meaning of the term "bad egg." Sadly, when it comes to the selection of good eggs, you have to place your trust in your supplier. For the only way to discover whether your eggs are good or bad is to crack them open. By and large, however, eggs generally obtained are of quite good quality. In fact, a danger lies in buying farm eggs which may have been too casually handled. When they are properly chosen and meticulously stored under refrigeration, farm eggs are the freshest and thus the best. On the other hand, the two occasions when I purchased bad eggs were times when the eggs were "fresh from the farm."

Grading of Eggs

All eggs are graded by standards set by the Department of Agriculture. "AA" are the finest—if you succeed in finding them. (They are available in better stores, sometimes sold under some local farm name without the grading noted on the carton.) These are for table use rather than for cooking. Grade "A" are for table use and cooking. These are the ones most of us are usually offered.

Grade "B" is the commercial standard—good for cooking but not, for instance, suitable for poaching or soft-boiling. If you select these eggs, it would be advisable to keep one of the higher grades in your refrigerator as well for table use. It is sometimes wisely frugal to purchase Grade "B" eggs for a special cooking task, but for the great majority of purposes, Grade "A" is preferable and safer.

Sizes of Eggs

    EXTRA LARGE: 27 ounces per dozen
    LARGE: 24 ounces per dozen
    MEDIUM: 21 ounces per dozen
    SMALL: 18 ounces per dozen
    PULLET: 15 ounces per dozen

Sizes of eggs are obtainable in all three grades.
If you feel that the eggs you've bought are underweight,

put two or three on a scale and multiply by the appropriate number. This is especially important when you're making a soufflé or a mousse. You may, of course, substitute two small eggs for one large one. I always use large eggs for cooking. I've never perceived the economy of buying small eggs. It takes 4 to 6 large eggs and 12 to 14 small ones to fill a standard measuring cup. (See Appendix I.) It is my suspicion that most eggs are sized inaccurately on the low side, i.e., not in the consumer's favor, a thought that will scarcely come as a surprise to many shoppers. The result is that I frequently add an egg or two to the quantity called for in a recipe, just to be on the safe side.

Color of Eggs

Though neither Americans nor Europeans can agree about this, it is a simple and demonstrable fact that the color of an eggshell has no relation whatever to the flavor or quality of its contents. Demand for either white or brown eggs is entirely a matter of local custom—superstition.

Storage of Eggs

A basket or rack of eggs may appear absolutely charming, but it is the wrong way to store them. Eggs should be kept in a closed carton or some other tight container in the refrigerator.

They shouldn't be washed. The shell is porous. The egg comes with a natural protective film that prevents it from picking up the odors of strong-flavored foods it may be stored beside.

Eggs should be used within a week or ten days of purchase. Even if you chance to keep them longer than that, they won't necessarily become "bad." But their powers may change—the capacity of the yolk to work as a thickening agent may decrease but the ability of the white to act as a leavening (raising) agent in dishes like angel food cake may increase.

You may keep yolks in a closed jar in your refrigerator for

a few days, provided that you cover them with a film of water, milk, or oil. (Choose the liquid according to the use to which you eventually mean to put the yolks.) Whites may be kept (by themselves, of course) for a week under similar conditions, or they may even be frozen in a plastic container. Be sure to keep track of the number of whites you are storing. They can't be counted after you've put them together.

How to Break an Egg

Even if you think yourself a skilled hand at breaking an egg, you'd be well advised when you want a whole egg to break it first into a saucer and then slip it into the pan; for if, by accident, you break the yolk, you can use another egg.

If, when you are separating eggs, a yolk should escape among the whites, wash and rinse your hands thoroughly (so that no oil from the soap is left on them), then grit your teeth and dip one hand into the whites, under the elusive yolk. Raise your hand slowly, splaying your fingers a little to allow the adhering white to drip back into the bowl.

If you are nervous when separating eggs, have ready three small bowls for the purpose, one for the whites, one for the yolks, and the other for the eggs that break. Then empty the contents of each into a larger container when the process has been completed.

It's important never to leave a drop of the yolk with the white. The fat contained in the yolk will inhibit the leavening power of the white. If this should occur, use a fragment of shell or a piece of paper toweling to retrieve it.

Bowls for Beating Egg Whites

The bowl traditionally used for the beating of whites is a specially shaped utensil made of unlined copper. The chemical action of the whites with copper makes this kind of receptacle best. For most of us, however, the use of a stainless steel bowl is perfectly acceptable; bowls of china or glass will also serve. *Don't* use a plastic bowl for beating whites (except when forced by your electrical equipment to do so), mainly because it is nearly impossible to be certain that a plastic utensil is entirely free of fat—and fat is the scourge of egg whites.

Eggs and Temperature

Eggs should *always* be used when they are at room temperature. It won't, of course, ruin your breakfast eggs if you prepare them directly from the refrigerator. But for any purpose where the egg is supposed to do something of real significance to a dish, it should be taken out of the refrigerator an hour or two ahead of time, so that its temperature is about 70°. The cold inhibits the capacity of the whites to achieve their greatest volume when beaten. Not being a chemist I can't explain this phenomenon, but I've observed it. If for some reason you need to use an egg and all your eggs are cold, immerse them in warm, *not* hot, water for 15 or 20 minutes. (If the water is too hot, you'll partially cook them.) If you fail to follow the room-temperature rule, something disastrous can occur, for eggs are extremely susceptible (even vulnerable) to heat. One of the most important things to understand about them is this touchiness with respect to temperature and to changes in temperature.

If subjected to excessive heat, the white becomes rubbery instead of just congealing. I'm sure you've had hard-boiled eggs that suffered from this condition.

If the yolk is exposed to too much heat, it becomes hard and powdery when used in a sauce or other liquid. The yolk (indeed, the entire egg) actually curdles. The scrambled egg will give you an idea of what happens, for scrambled eggs are merely curdled eggs that have been organized.

Even when you are cooking breakfast eggs, it is advisable to prepare them at as leisurely a pace as your time limitations allow.

To avoid curdling eggs when you are using them for a sauce, employ a double boiler or set the pot containing the eggs in a pan or skillet of hot water (making a sort of informal *bain-marie*). *Don't* allow the water to come to a boil, regardless of which method you use. More attention is required with the *bain-marie* method than with a double boiler because in the former instance the bottom of the pan is close to the heating surface of the stove.

When using the oven for the preparation of eggs, as in custards, set the dish containing the eggs in a pan of hot water on the bottom shelf. This works like a double boiler, protecting the bottom of the custard against excessive heat. The temperature setting should be 325°–350°.

If you don't use a pan of water, as in the case of baked eggs or *quiche,* you should still place the utensil on the bottom shelf, employing the same basically moderate temperature setting—though a slightly higher temperature may be applied at the beginning. Your recipe should furnish this kind of direction.

MAGIC WITH EGGS

Both yolks and whites may be used for purposes of thickening. Sometimes they can be deployed in combination. However, as in the instances of soufflés, mousses, sauces, and some puddings, they do a better job when used separately.

If whole eggs are to be employed as thickeners (they are in custards), beat them enough to mix the whites and yolks. Overbeating makes them foamy and will cause bubbles of egg to float to the surface of the mixture instead of combining with it.

However, when you are using egg yolks to thicken soups or sauces or mixtures that are hot, you should beat the yolks vigorously, adding some of the hot mixture and often cream or evaporated milk to the egg yolks before you combine them with the mixture itself. Then slowly pour them into the main dish, stirring as you do. Once the eggs have been introduced into a dish, *never* allow this combination to come to a boil.

Eggs as Emulsifying Agents
You can blend two liquids which won't combine independently by the addition of raw egg yolks; they will serve as emulsifiers.

Eggs as Binding Agents
As the yolk of egg is used in the making of tempera color to cause dry pigment to set, so are the yolk and the whole egg employed internally to cause a hash, a meat loaf, or potatoes to cohere; they are used externally to make flour, bread crumbs, or cornmeal adhere to the surface of a mixture or a piece of food you plan to fry.

Eggs to Add Body and Strength
The gluing quality of the yolk and the whole egg helps to hold flour and butter together when you are making pastry, so you can roll it out repeatedly and compose a good, tender, but sturdy crust.

Eggs in Glazing
Eggs beaten with water and brushed on the surface of bread and pastry before baking give them a brilliant glaze.

Eggs in Clarifying
Beaten egg whites, when stirred into a boiling stock, attract the tiny particles of material which you'll want to remove. Both the whites and particles are easily eliminated from the stock by pouring it through a fine strainer or piece of cheesecloth.

Eggs as Leavening Agents
The propensity of egg whites to "blow up" when they are beaten is increased by the judicious introduction of heat

and air. This tendency to expand is enhanced in an oven. The bubbles of air become fixed in the baking process. You can perceive this action in the manufacture of a soufflé, sponge cake, and angel food cake.

Some Tips for the Use of Egg Whites
- If used at room temperature, as noted above, egg whites will beat better and rise more completely, forming air bubbles of more uniform size than if processed cold.

- A pinch of salt, introduced as you beat, will increase the rising action of the whites. You must, however, exercise discretion. Too much salt will eliminate the elasticity of the whites and cause the mixture to break down.

- When the whites reach the foamy stage, the addition of cream of tartar or a small quantity of lemon juice will augment their volume and make them more stable. Either of these additions also makes for a lighter and whiter mixture of egg whites.

- When adding sugar to egg whites, be sure to do it after the beating has taken you past the foamy stage and the mixture has attained a good bulk. Sugar and other sweeteners protect the structure of the froth and make it less vulnerable to overbeating.

- Egg whites must be beaten immediately before using.

Beating Egg Whites
Using an egg beater or whisk, beat egg whites just to the point where, when you lift out the beater, they will form a straight but soft peak that gleams. This description may seem inadequate, but it is exact, all the same. If the peaks are too stiff and dry and lusterless, it means the whites have been beaten too much. Only after getting some experience with looking at beaten whites in various stages can you be sure. The following pointers, however, may prove helpful:

- You test for peaks by slowly removing the beater, which will pull the egg whites into peaks.

- In the case of angel food cake, you want your peaks to bend over slightly at the top. In other words, the whites should not be so thoroughly beaten as would be necessary for a mousse, soufflé, or other kind of cake.

- The bubbles should be of uniform size. If they are not, continue beating. Underbeaten whites can't "hold up" the ingredients you plan to mix with them.

- When correctly beaten, egg whites should move very slowly if you turn the bowl almost completely upside down.

Folding

Folding is the process by which you combine egg whites with another mixture. In this process you are trying to knock as little air as possible out of the whites. If you have removed too much air, you will discover the fact when you serve it, for it will not be so light as you would like it to be.

TECHNIQUES OF FOLDING

To begin the folding process, mix a generous spoonful of egg white into the batter or sauce with which it is to be blended, then pour the mixture into the bowl of whites.

For folding, hold the stirring spoon as nearly horizontal as possible and insert it just below the surface of the mixture, using a motion rather like that of scything, beginning at one edge of the bowl and working toward the other, dipping slightly into the material as you go, maintaining a flat oval movement back and forth. The back of your hand, upward at the start of the passage, turns slowly in a clockwise direction as you reach the other side. Then raise the spoon, turn your wrist so the back of your hand again faces upward, and repeat the process. Always keep the spoon nearly horizontal. These movements are continued until the egg whites are fully blended with the rest of the mixture.

If you have a large French wooden spatula, you'll find it very useful for folding. Otherwise, use a shallow-bowled wooden spoon.

EGG COOKERY

Often when critics say of a novice, "She doesn't know how to boil water," they're likely to add, "She doesn't know how to boil an egg." Well, as it happens, boiling an egg properly (soft or hard) is a very tricky aspect of egg cookery. This is something you appreciate only after you have been served a perfectly boiled egg, a delicately delicious object.

Boiled Eggs
SOFT-BOILED EGGS

Here are some rules of thumb. They are not ironclad, because personal preferences are involved:

- If the egg to be soft-boiled is at room temperature before you start cooking it, place it in a small pot and generously cover it with cold water, at least ½ cup of water per egg. Bring it to a boil, then allow it to simmer for 90 seconds. This method is for use if the egg is to be brought to the table and allowed to wait a few moments before it is eaten, for it will continue to cook after it has been removed from the simmering water. However, if the egg is to be consumed as soon as it is served, the technique is slightly different. It should be simmered for 2 to 2½ minutes, then held under the cold water tap for a few seconds to arrest the cooking process and to cool the shell.

- When you are going to boil an egg that has come directly from the refrigerator, use exactly the same process as noted above, adding 30 seconds to each of the operations described.

- The size of the pot, the amount of water it contains, and the number of eggs to be boiled at one time will affect—upward or downward—the times I've suggested. Until you've done your own experiments with pots and quantities, you'll be somewhat in the dark about precise timings, for these also depend on the degree of firmness you like in your soft-boiled eggs.
- One final point. Do *not* boil eggs in an aluminum pot. The process will stain it. It won't have any bad effect on the egg, however, so if you don't care about staining the pot, forget this tip.
- A different but quite satisfactory method of soft-boiling eggs, whether at room temperature or straight from the refrigerator, is to plunge them into a pot that is generously full of boiling water and allow them to cook for 2½ to 4 minutes, according to your taste. Then cool them under cold running water.

HARD-BOILED EGGS

Whether at room temperature or fresh from the refrigerator, hard-cooked eggs should be started in cold water, then brought to a boil and allowed to simmer for 12 minutes. Then plunge them into cold water as soon as you have removed them from the stove.

To peel a hard-cooked egg, knock it gently on its rounder end (where the air bubble is) and roll the shell gently on a hard surface with the palm of your hand, cracking it as you do. A single perforation of the inner skin will make it easy to peel. If you encounter bits of shell that resist this method, complete the job under running water. The fresher the egg, the harder it will be to peel.

Fried Eggs

Use a frying pan of a size adequate for the number of eggs you plan to fry at one time. Place one tablespoon of grease in the pan for each egg. The material employed may be bacon fat, butter, or some other oil whose flavor you like. Heat it in the pan. When the oil is hot, break each egg into a saucer, then slip it from the saucer into the frying pan. Turn down the heat. Spoon the hot fat over the top of the egg until it is fried to your taste. If your preference is for "once over lightly," flip the egg gently with a spatula and allow it to fry in the upside-down position for only a few seconds.

FRENCH-FRIED EGGS

Half fill a small saucepan with oil (preferably olive oil). When it is very hot, slip the egg from a saucer into the hot oil. Do this gingerly, for the oil will bubble up when it comes into contact with the cool egg. Cook until the egg rises to the surface.

Scrambled Eggs
METHOD 1: FRYING PAN METHOD

Allow two or three eggs per serving. Beat the eggs in a bowl with a fork, adding one tablespoon of cream, milk, or water and a pinch each of salt and pepper. Heat a tablespoon of butter per serving in a frying pan. When the butter is hot but not yet brown, add the eggs and reduce the heat. Stir the eggs constantly with a wooden spoon until *almost* done. Remove them. The cooking will be finished by the heat which the eggs retain. That's a significant measure of their extreme sensitivity.

METHOD 2: SQUIGGLED EGGS

This is a dish named by June Platt. Break the eggs into a bowl. Heat butter in a frying pan as in Method 1. Slip the eggs into the pan and break the yolks while you are stirring the eggs with a wooden spoon. Remove them from the heat just before they are completely cooked. If you are not careful about this, they'll be dried out before you serve them. A flavor richer than the one obtained with Method 1 results.

METHOD 3: SCRAMBLING IN A DOUBLER BOILER

This is the most savory and also the richest of scrambled egg recipes. It also takes the longest time to prepare. It requires, as noted, the use of a double boiler. Bring the water in the bottom of the double boiler to a boil to warm the upper portion. Place a large chunk of butter in the top section. When the butter has melted, turn down the heat a bit. Add the eggs, still stirring them (as in Method 1), switching to a wire whisk which you must use constantly. Add more butter, still stirring. When the eggs are done, they will of course be very buttery and have a consistency of little clusters—unctuous, creamy, and much smoother than the results obtained with the two other methods.

Shirred Eggs

Use small, circular shirred-egg dishes for this preparation. Heat the oven to 350°. Melt some butter or place partially cooked bacon in the bottom of each dish. Then introduce one or two eggs to each, adding a knob of butter on top, and bake them on the oven's bottom shelf until the white has just set—about 15 minutes. Remove from the oven, season with salt and pepper, and serve.

Poached Eggs

For poaching you may use a frying pan, a gratin dish, or any other utensil at least 3 inches deep. If you heavily butter the interior, it will be easier to clean.

Fill the pan with water, adding a substantial dash of vinegar, which helps to congeal the whites. Carefully slide each egg, one by one, into the boiling water. Slip a pancake turner under each to be certain that none is touching the bottom of the pan. With a spoon, flick water over the tops of the eggs. Depending on your taste, the cooking time will vary from 3 to 5 minutes. Remove the eggs from the water with a slotted wooden spoon. Place them on a folded towel to dry.

If you're greatly concerned about the appearance of your poached eggs, you have two alternatives—to purchase a poacher which has small molds for each egg, or to trim the edges of each egg after it has been poached, a tedious business. I'm not so fond of the molded poached egg as of the natural kind, and I don't think it necessary to trim them.

Oeufs Mollet

This is a method of preparing eggs that is frequently used in French dishes. Eggs must be at room temperature. Plunge them into boiling water, then reduce the heat until the water is just below a simmer. Cook them for 6 minutes. Then immerse the eggs in cold water and peel them as you would hard-boiled eggs. The difference between this and the normal hard-boiled egg is that the yolk remains soft.

You may keep the eggs warm after peeling by putting them in hot, not boiling, water.

Omelets

Yes, you really have to have a proper omelet pan, a utensil which is only wiped, not washed, after each use, and conditioned with salt. However, a Teflon-coated pan will do—though it won't last you a lifetime, thus becoming like a dear old friend.

Taking into consideration the size of your pan, break an appropriate number of eggs—never more then eight—into a mixing bowl. Beat them for about a minute with a fork, stirring in a pinch of salt.

Place a heaping tablespoon of butter into the omelet pan. Let it heat until it begins to brown and smells nutlike.

Give your eggs one more rapid beating and pour them into the pan, turning it from side to side so that the eggs cover the whole cooking surface.

Stir the eggs quickly. Turn the heat down a bit, and with a spatula carefully lift one edge of the omelet, allowing some of the uncooked egg to run underneath. Do this three or four times, being sure to leave some uncooked egg on the surface.

The degree of the omelet's dryness is a matter of taste. When yours has achieved the state you desire, fold it. If it is a small one, do this by bending it in half. If it is large, fold the two sides toward the center, then flip it upside down onto a warm platter. Traditionally, an omelet should be moist in the center.

When you're making other than plain omelets, be guided by your recipe. Sometimes you'll mix the other ingredients with the egg before the beginning of the cooking process. On other occasions, you'll make a stuffing which is placed on the omelet just prior to folding it.

EGGS IN COMBINATION WITH OTHER INGREDIENTS

Liquid Custard

This is composed of eggs, sugar, milk, cream, and flavoring. Eggs are employed as a thickening agent, so they shouldn't be beaten more than is necessary to make them combine with the sugar and milk. Liquid custard should be cooked in a *bain-marie* or a double boiler. It is finished when a silver spoon emerges well coated. The water may boil, but only gently. A little patience is required to achieve the desired thickness. Add cold water in the bottom of the double boiler as the boiling water evaporates. If you start with eggs at room temperature, the thickening will be hastened.

Custards, Quiches, *and Puddings*

In all of these dishes, as with liquid custard, eggs are used as a thickening agent, so don't overbeat them. This will prevent the formation of bubbles in a preparation whose consistency should be exceptionally smooth.

Bake a *quiche* on the bottom shelf of your oven. A *quiche* need not be placed in a pan of water. Its moisture is preserved by its crust.

Place your custard dish in a pan of hot water on the oven's lowest level also. Oven temperatures should be provided with your recipe. A custard is cooked when a silver knife emerges clean after insertion into its center.

Soufflés, Mousses, and Quenelles

The mousse, the soufflé, and the *quenelle* are cousins. A soufflé—a mixture of flavored cream sauce with eggs—is generally served hot. It can be served plain or with such flavorings as vanilla, chocolate, a liqueur, or finely minced meat, vegetables, or cheese. The selected ingredient is folded in with egg whites and baked. (Always provide one more egg white than yolk, unless this is already specified in your recipe.) Be sure your dish is not too large for the batter mixture. Otherwise, your soufflé will fail to rise above the top.

A mousse is a sauce made of uncooked whole eggs, to which may be added a variety of finely chopped ingredients or flavorings, beaten egg whites, whipped cream, and often gelatin. Time is required for the mousse to "set"—that is, to dry out. If the weather is humid, you should allow twice the time for this than you would under dry conditions. Cold soufflé more closely resembles a mousse than a soufflé.

The French *quenelle* is a sort of egg dumpling which is poached in stock or a *fumet*.

In all of these preparations, the yolk of the egg is used as a binding and/or leavening agent; the white is exclusively for leavening.

TECHNIQUES OF PREPARING MOUSSES AND SOUFFLÉS

In the preparation of a mousse or a soufflé, add the yolks to the sauce after it comes from the stove and has had a chance to cool a bit. It *must* be cool before you fold in the egg whites. Be sure to add a touch of the beaten white to the egg-yolk mixture before beginning the folding process (described earlier in this section). The directions given earlier for adding a pinch of salt and cream of tartar to egg whites apply to soufflés.

A collar of foil or cooking paper, well buttered, will help stabilize and give a picture-book appearance to your soufflé. Do not expect to see a very abundant soufflé if your soufflé dish is too large for the quantity to be cooked.

Soufflés are placed in a pan of boiling water and baked on the middle shelf of the oven, which should be set at 375°–400°. You must restrain your curiosity about the soufflé's progress for at least 20 minutes.

Find the recipe you have the best luck with and stick to it. I recommend the one in *The Kitchen Scholar*. A dear friend who is a fine cook swears by Julia Child's formula. Whatever the recipe, don't peek for 20 minutes or you'll risk disaster—the collapse of the soufflé.

8

The Imperative: *Soups*

A True Story About False Teeth

Long ago, in New York, when I could still be described as a bride, my husband Donald invited an elderly explorer, Robert Dunn, to come to our apartment for the afternoon to discuss the prospect of an editing job and to stay on for dinner. The morning of the day set for the meeting, Dunn called to say that he couldn't stay for dinner because, as he'd been getting out of bed that morning, he'd stepped on his false teeth and shattered them and would consequently be unable to eat anything solid. I assured him that I could provide a meal that required no chewing: lobster bisque.

We had been introduced to lobster bisque a couple of years before, when we were living in Brussels. Then, as now, I think it one of the most delicious soups and—teeth or no teeth—a most suitable dish for an honored guest. But what would I serve to follow it? A cheese soufflé—not an ordinary one, but a soufflé prepared with Parmesan cheese. For dessert, I planned pears in port, slightly overcooked to make them easy on Dunn's gums. I was delighted with this menu; it was carefully thought out, balanced, and worth at least one of the *Guide Michelin*'s stars for quality, three for consideration.

By the time Donald and Bobby Dunn were settled in our living room discussing the work that had to be done in order to make his extraordinary memoirs publishable, I had researched my cookbooks and completed my marketing. The apartment was one of those old railroad flats. The kitchen adjoined the living room, so I was able to listen to the two men as I cooked. Since the *magnum opus* was the bisque, I set to work on it first.

All the recipes I'd consulted were in agreement about the manufacture of lobster bisque: Sauté the raw lobster in butter. When the shell turned red, I should flambé it with brandy. That seemed simple enough. Then I had to remove the meat from the shell and set it aside. The next step was, literally and figuratively, the crunch: I had to pulverize the shells, for lobster shell serves as part of the bisque, adding color and density as well as flavor. But how did one go about pulverizing them?

I broke the shells into small pieces and put a few into a large brass mortar (which was equipped with a formidable brass pestle) and started to crush them. My working surface was a slab of marble that served as a counter top. The very first stroke of the pestle produced thunderous reverberations in the kitchen. I put a dish towel under the mortar to muffle at least the more resonating of the sounds. It didn't help much. Then I tried to grind the shells in the mortar, using slow, forceful pressure on the pestle. But the result was no appreciable improvement.

Donald entered the kitchen, doing his best to appear

calm, but there was blood in his eye. What the hell did I think I was doing? I explained a bit defensively, knowing in my heart that the dinner was really the most important part of Dunn's visit. Donald, however, obviously felt that his business conversation was the paramount issue.

There was an impasse. The poor men simply sat back, staring at the ceiling, while I completed the orgy of banging and crashing. They were finally able to resume their talk. The meal was a great success. Donald didn't get the editorial job, but I refuse to believe that the noise of the crunching lobster shells had anything to do with it. Dunn had a prior commitment to another free-lance writer.

Weeks afterward, Nell Boni, a dear friend whose husband Albert had recommended Donald to Bobby Dunn, asked how the meeting had gone off. I described what had happened. Nell is Dutch, and a fine cook. Like the Belgians, the Dutch are very fond of lobster bisque. So I asked her if there was a way of pulverizing the shells without making all that racket. Her reply was so obvious that I felt like applying that pestle to my head. "Dry the shells in a warm oven for two or three hours before you crush them. They turn to powder the way dry bread does."

SOUPS

Nothing starts off a dinner party with more *éclat* than a soup, and especially with today's high food prices, it is thrifty to serve a preliminary course. Certainly, it takes a little more time. But in the case of soups, they can always be made a day ahead. As with casseroles and stews, they are often better for a day's delay in serving, for their flavors have had an opportunity to ripen together for 24 hours or so.

Later in this section I shall deal with the various types of soups. I can do no more here than allude to those from which to make a selection—there is a library of books devoted exclusively to this subject. Here I want to generalize about the serving of soup.

Serving Soups

When serving soup as a first course, there are a couple of things you should keep in mind. Like many other appetizers, you can have it on the table when your guests are seated. If you have warmed the soup bowls and served the soup very hot, it should be at a satisfactory temperature. An alternative that takes a little more time (but assures that it is hot) is to ladle it into the bowls after your friends are actually at the table. Another is to present a soup intended to be eaten at room temperature.

Most cold soups, except when served on the hottest of evenings, are preferable when cool—not chilled. A soup that is too cold loses its taste. There are many cold soups, like vichyssoise and its numerous cousins, that can be presented year-round. A cold borscht isn't just a summer soup, either.

Some hot soups should only be served in winter—cheddar cheese soup, onion soup (marvelous before steak), bean soup, and hot borscht, to cite only a few of the literally countless varieties.

Nor should we forget the "seasonal" soups, those prepared with fresh vegetables—fresh pea or asparagus or tomato. These may all be served cold as well as hot. While gazpacho, the great Spanish vegetable soup, can only be served cold, there are numerous hot vegetable soups—"green soups," like minestrone or pistou—to offer an embarrassment of choices.

The service of certain kinds of soup will dictate what you present in subsequent courses. For instance, if you offer a vegetable soup, hot or cold, it may be superfluous to add vegetables to the main portion of the meal, whether cooked or as salad.

Finally, there are soups that are meals in themselves, like bouillabaisse, the gift of Marseilles to the culinary world. After presenting this, all you need add is a salad and dessert—nothing more. The *pot au feu*, mentioned earlier on, is another instance. Nothing is more popular in my own family (or for frequent intimates) than a great pot of rich soup served with bread, cheese, and followed by a simple dessert.

I think you will find, as I have, that men are almost as fond of soup as they are of steak. This may come as a surprise to both sexes!

Many soups can be satisfactorily frozen. The only significant problem I've found is with the freezing of soups that contain pieces of potato; their texture becomes unpleasantly coarse when thawed. However, a purée which has been previously frozen, then laced with cream before serving, is always delicious. (For details about effective freezing, consult a book devoted to this subject on which I don't consider myself at all expert.)

As you read recipes in American and European cookbooks, you will find many soups that require less than an hour to make, from start to finish, *including* the time involved in preparing the ingredients. Research will show that many of the finest soups don't call for the use of stock; you need only plain water. The number of quickly made vegetable soups, however, will *double* if you have availed yourself of the opportunity to make stocks and *roux* ahead of time, at your convenience.

Once you have tasted some of the soups you can make in your own kitchen without too great an effort, you may never want to employ another canned or freeze-dried variety again—except in an emergency.

Let me once again attempt to dispel the myth about the great soup pot that sits on the back of your stove, improving as the days and weeks and months elapse. It's just not true. A good vegetable soup is impregnated with the flavor of *fresh* vegetables that have just been cooked—and cooked until they are just done, not cooked to death.

Equipment

It is not merely a boon but really a necessity to have the proper equipment for soupmaking:

A large pot, preferably of enameled cast iron
A colander
A large sieve
A food mill
A blender
A mandolin grater

A great help is a spider-legged Mouli-brand grater for chopping vegetables.

If you play your cards right, you may induce someone who loves you to present you with that kitchen wonder, a Braun or Hobart Kitchen Machine. It won't cook for you, but it will certainly make kitchen chores much easier by grating, mincing, chopping, blending, and mixing.

A blender should be used with some caution. For example, a cold vichyssoise can be mixed to a perfect smoothness in a blender. But a watercress soup or a purée of vegetables is over-refined by the use of such an appliance. The food mill, though it is operated by hand, will give a heartier, less effete texture appropriate to the material. It is in these terms that the cook should think when determining which of the available machines and utensils should be used for a particular job: Should the soup be unctuous or hearty?

TYPES OF SOUPS

The basic varieties of soups are:

Clear soup
Purée
Thick soup (including *velouté* and bisque)
Classic vegetable soup

Clear Soups

The preparation of clear soups is similar to that for making stocks. You may use meat, poultry, fish (and shellfish),

Types of Soups 123

and game. If the essence is meat, you'll add aromatic vegetables. The ingredients vary from recipe to recipe.

Clear soups require the longest time to prepare, for you must allow time for the essence of the fundamental ingredient to be extracted from meat and bones. A good rich stock is, after all, nothing more or less than a clear soup. As a rough estimate, an average clear soup requires something like 3 or 4 hours to make. However, as I've remarked before, not by any means is your physical presence or attention required for *all* of this time; you can be doing other tasks while the soup is in preparation.

Clear soups, consommés, and bouillons are named either for their essence (chicken, beef, etc.) or for the ingredient added to the essence in the final stages of its cooking. Aurora, for example, is a chicken consommé with tomato purée added as a thickener.

To my taste, the greatest of all clear soups, and one of the most useful, is the broth that results from the preparation of *pot au feu;* this is called *petite marmite* or *potage Henri IV,* depending on the variety of vegetables added. The reward from a *pot au feu* is considerable, as I noted in the section devoted to stocks.

Purées

In this category are all the soups which are smoothed and/or thickened at the conclusion of the cooking process by the use of a blender or a food mill.

Purées are generally thickened by the refinement of the potatoes with which they are made. They are often finished by the addition of egg yolk as a binder, with which cream or canned evaporated milk may be mixed for smoothness and final blending. A touch of butter stirred in at the very end sets everything up.

Cream and butter are optional ingredients for a purée. Salt and pepper are not; inadequate quantities of these spices can appreciably impair the result.

Purées of beans, lentils, or dried peas do not need potatoes or egg yolks for thickening—though you may want to add a little cream or canned milk at the end. Again, these niceties depend on the recipe you follow. Some call for sautéed aromatic vegetables, for instance. A split pea soup cooked with a ham bone will take longer to prepare. A delicious purée can be made with nothing but vegetables, a few herbs, and water, cooked just long enough to make the vegetables tender; then you purée it and serve with grated cheese. This is quick to make, good, and cheap.

Satisfying purées of all descriptions are easy to prepare and, consequently, very worthwhile. Like stews, they are quite frequently tastier when served a day after they're made because their ingredients have been permitted more time to blend. Moreover, with the addition of little more than a loaf of good bread or some rolls, you'll find that a purée can represent an entire meal, it is so filling. And if you plan to serve a meat course afterward, you'll happily discover that your guests' appetites have been much reduced—which, given the astronomical prices of meat, isn't a bad eventuality.

Thick Soups

This category includes cream soups, bisques, and *veloutés*.

A cream soup may be made with fish, poultry, or vegetables, together with a white sauce (for thickness) and milk, instead of stock. It is to be finished with cream—sometimes egg yolks and butter are required.

Bisque consists of the meat (and sometimes the shell) of shellfish, together with a *mirepoix*. It is thickened with rice, or occasionally with bread or a white *roux* that has been thinned with fish stock. At the end of the preparation, egg yolks and cream are added. The only caution to note is one of which I was once ignorant: Dry the shells in the oven before pulverizing them!

The *veloutés* are the most formidable of the thick soups in terms of variety. They may be made with vegetables, poultry, game, or fish. An example is a white *roux* (thinned with stock of chicken, veal, or fish—depending on the main ingredient of the soup), together with essence of mushroom or vegetable. I especially like a veal stock with celery or celeriac (knob celery) or some other vegetable with a strong flavor. For this purpose, I find the chicken stock too light. All *veloutés* are normally finished with egg yolks and cream.

PREPARATION OF VELOUTÉ

The main ingredient, well minced, should be sautéed in butter until soft.

The combination of *roux* and stock is added, allowing the mixture to cook until done—not very long.

Put the contents through a sieve or mix in a blender.

Bind with egg yolks and cream.

Give the result the blessing of a touch of butter for added unctuousness, being sure to check that you've added enough salt and pepper. (White pepper is inconspicuous in pale soups.) You might save a few tidbits of the main ingredient of the soup to use as a garnish.

Special Soups

Into this classification fall all the soups that really are meals in themselves—the French *garbure,* various European peasant soups (like minestrone), and American chowders. (Incidentally, it is something of a surprise to discover that the origin of the word "chowder" is the French *"chaudière"* —a boiling pot, the term and the pot having traveled to New England from French Canada.)

The general pattern for the preparation of these soups is the same: They consist of various vegetables, starchy products, diced meat, seafood, or poultry, sautéed in wine, stock, water, or milk until *just* done, and served as they are.

I'm sure that you could discover a different special soup for every day of the year—and be the better for it.

If you decide to prepare a soup from leftovers, I implore you to stick to the same group of rules I've outlined here, depending on the category that is applicable. A marvelous soup can be made, for example, from leftover spinach and milk in a blender. Mushroom peels can be simmered in water until they've given up all their essence—then are sieved to make a delicious broth.

Infinite and infinitely rewarding indeed are the pleasures of soupmaking.

9

Qualifying Phrases: *Sauces, the Consummate Achievement of Cooking*

On Hating Sauces

Nothing more rapidly widens the horizons of a cook's repertory than mastery of a few great sauces. And once a family has been introduced to the habit of sauces, you'll never again be allowed to return to the routine of sauceless dishes. For all concerned, mealtimes assume a new dimension of pleasure—and you, as cook, will enjoy yourself increasingly as you widen your knowledge of saucemaking and as the process grows simpler through experience.

I'm always infuriated by the individual (usually a man) who claims belligerently that he hates sauces. The tone of the observation often seems to invite you, who *love* sauces, to believe that there is something odd about you. Yet almost invariably it turns out that in an even more stentorian tone he calls for ketchup, Worcestershire sauce, Heinz "57," or another of the extremely complicated sauces that one can't attempt to produce in a home kitchen. This is the same fellow who adds extra mayonnaise to his sandwiches.

The fact is that no one hates *all* sauces and, as a rule, the sauces the "sauce-hater" hates are merely those with which he is not familiar; he has no objection to the sophistication or flavor of these sauces. His mother neglected his education in the real refinements of eating.

Although those observations are demonstrably accurate, the logic of truth seldom wins an emotional argument. One can't successfully fight food prejudice with reason any more than one can prevail by this route against racism or nationalism. How, then, does one seduce the diehard?

Let's examine the nature of the sauces that can be made at home, beginning with the simplest and working up to the most elaborate. If you accustom yourself to saucemaking and incorporate sauces into your normal routine of cooking, you may surprise and stimulate your sauce-hater—and eventually succeed in purchasing fewer of the prepared varieties. For your own satisfaction, you'll soon be using them to add zest and interest to your dishes. Be sure to write down the recipe of a sauce that is successful, so you're able to remind yourself to use it again when the proper moment arrives.

SAUCES: HOMOGENEOUS AND CONTRASTING

Whether complicated or simple, there are really only two sorts of sauce: those that are homogeneous and those that are contrasting. Though there are homogeneous sauces that are complex, the easiest of all sauces to make is one employing the drippings and residue in the pan of either a sauté or a roast.

The contrasting sauces are made with materials other

than those of the dish they accompany, and they constitute a much broader range than the homogeneous group, starting with the simple ones (consisting of a single fundamental operation) and ending with the combination sauces, which can be extremely complex. Sometimes their flavors are related to the dishes they are to be served with, sometimes they are in total contrast, yet they are *always* complementary, a good marriage of tastes, like vanilla ice cream with chocolate sauce. (Yet even with so basic an example as this one, interesting variations are possible—like the addition to chocolate sauce of an orange liqueur, orange juice, or grated orange rind; a little more effort, really, but the usual is thus made unusual.)

Preparing a Homogeneous Sauce

If there is a lot of fat, you must remove some of it, leaving perhaps a tablespoonful. Then you "wash" it—add a cup or so of some hot liquid and bring it to a boil, stirring in all the residue. Add some salt and pepper and parsley, and it's done. The hot liquid may be stock related to the main dish, or it may be wine, or even water. If the notion pleases you, add a dash of Tabasco, Worcestershire, or one of the other prepared savory sauces—but try the plain liquids first.

It is not possible to furnish useful measurements, because each sauce of this sort depends on the size of your pan, what you've cooked as your main course, and the number of people to be served. It is important, in any event, to add the supplementary liquid carefully, for you must boil it down to the point where it has a good strong flavor. If you've used a *mirepoix* or a *matignon*, strain these vegetables out *after* having added your liquid and used them further to give flavor to your sauce.

There are other ways of improvising on this simple sauce. If you've not made a *mirepoix* or *matignon*, you may sauté some onions, shallots, or scallions in the residue in your pan. All should be very finely chopped for this purpose. For the sauce-maker, the shallot is the finest member of the onion family, the one you'll use most frequently for the purpose, if you can obtain it. Scallions are my second choice for sauces, onions a distinct third.

Whether you've made a *mirepoix* or not, you may want to add mushrooms, precooked in a little water, or blanched olives. They may be used together, as well. Even skinned tomatoes or tomato paste is useful in certain applications.

The point here is that the possible combinations are nearly infinite. You can make many delicious sauces whose distinctive flavor is determined by the choice of wine, fortified wine, brandy, or my friend Madeira (all preheated). Sometimes with ham or chicken, the addition of a tablespoon of jelly and a little mustard (of the prepared mustards, I prefer those from Dijon) will provide a unique taste. Fresh or sour cream are also important sauce ingredients at times.

If you want to thicken a homogeneous sauce, my own preference as agent is *beurre manié*—but only for fish, because with fish the sauce must furnish the body that the main dish itself lacks. To thicken a simple homogeneous sauce to which I've added cream, I use egg yolks. You can also compose a *roux*, using the pan grease as the base—but *I* wouldn't since it makes gravy.

Let me say a word about the virtues of the thin, natural sauce, as distinguished from those awful thickened gravies. They can be tasty. They are very easy to make. They are the mainstay of my day-to-day saucemaking. I feel their thin texture is far more compatible with meat.

Preparing a Contrasting Sauce

By "contrasting" sauces, I refer here to those that are not homogeneous, and the balance of the chapter is devoted to these. I am basing the discussion on French sauces mainly for reasons of space, but also because the processes of making sauces are essentially similar regardless of nationality. My hope is to provide a basis for all saucemaking by treating the French types. American sauces are improved by using their French cousins.

A good sauce should be smooth. In general, you start with a thickening agent—starch, egg yolks, etc.—and proceed to embellish it. The sauce should have body without seeming heavy (whether we are talking about mayonnaise or hard sauce). It shouldn't be as thick as, for example, mashed potatoes. It should flow quite freely. And while even the simplest sauce should add a distinctive flavor, this should be subtle without being insipid. No single flavor element should suppress the others in the composition of a sauce, and a sauce should not kill the basic flavor of the dish. You must attempt to achieve an ideal: a balance of all the essences that have gone into the preparation.

Equipment

Small but heavy metal saucepans are necessary; the flimsier ones lend themselves too easily to the burning of their contents. As in previous chapters, I recommend copper or, in its place, enameled cast iron.

You should also have a couple of doll-sized pots. For these, you might indulge yourself by purchasing a small set of copper pans such as are often found in gift shops; they can be useful as well as decorative. You need them for heating such liquids as vinegar, lemon juice, and spirits.

You must have some wooden spoons of sizes appropriate to the pans you're using, and you *ought* to have two double boilers of different capacities. One of them ought to be very small, like those used to heat baby food, ideal for family-sized quantities of sauce. My own is of white enamel and a constant joy.

You need two sizes of whisks, or one of the substitutes mentioned in an earlier section, twigs or spatulas.

A final must is a flame-tamer or trivet that will help control the heat of your burner (especially if you're cooking with gas).

TYPES OF SAUCES

Basic Brown Sauce

Though quite similar to the homogeneous sauce described earlier in this chapter, the difference is that you begin with a saucepan or double boiler, depending on how sure of yourself you are. You then make a brown *roux* which must be liquefied with brown stock or, if you *must,* canned bouillon or beef cubes, salt, and pepper. This sauce is normally used as is, occasionally dressed up a bit for service with sweetbreads or a dark-meat fish. The reason for its inclusion here is that it is the basic sauce used as the vehicle for some of the notable combinations, like *sauce bordelaise.*

If you already have a *roux* on hand, you'll only need to add the hot stock, stirring it in with a wire whisk, until you attain the desired consistency. Brown sauce should simmer for 30 minutes. Unless the recipe you are following stipulates otherwise, the proportions of fat and flour and liquid are 3 tablespoons of fat, 3 tablespoons of flour, and 2 cups of liquid. (It is a good idea to keep a tablespoon measure in your flour container for just such purposes.) An onion, shallots, or scallions may be added as well. If you elect to do this, you should start by sautéing them in the fat, then add flour and finally stock. Normally, this combination is strained before service.

BROWN SAUCE MADE WITH CORNSTARCH

Blend the cornstarch with cold stock (or canned bouillon), then add salt and pepper. Place the pan on a flame-tamer and cook it until it has thickened and become clear. Continue to simmer for 30 minutes, stirring frequently. *Don't boil it!*

SAUCE BOURGUIGNONNE

Sauce bourguignonne is made with wine, mushrooms, parsley, onions, shallots (or scallions), thyme, and bay leaf.

The proportions will be furnished in your cookbook. Boil these ingredients until the original contents of the pan have been reduced by half. Strain, and then thicken the liquid with a suitable amount of *beurre manié*. Cook it once again on low heat, stirring until it thickens. *Sauce bourguignonne* can be used on meats that have been roasted, sautéed, broiled, or blanched. It is also good with a dark-meat fish, eggs, such meat by-products as brains and sweetbreads, and with fowl.

An interesting and rapid variant of this is to make a brown sauce with fish stock instead of brown stock; this is usable with dishes that aren't seafood at all, with admirable results.

White Sauces
SAUCE VELOUTÉ

This is a white *roux* liquefied with veal, poultry, or fish stock, to which salt, white pepper, and a hint of cayenne pepper have been added. It is used on creamed chicken, on veal, or as a sauce for sole, halibut, and similarly bland varieties of fish. The type of stock you choose dictates its application. It may also be used on vegetables, but *sauce béchamel* is a better choice for this purpose. *Sauce velouté* will also tolerate the addition of cheese.

SAUCE BÉCHAMEL

This is also made from a base of white *roux* liquefied with veal, poultry, or fish stock (or with milk, cream, or a combination of stock and cream), salt, and the same peppers used for *sauce velouté*. I *always* add the cayenne, which makes the finished product hotter, adding to its character. As with a brown stock, you may add an onion or carrot. In general, you follow the procedure for making brown sauce.

Cheese is added according to purpose, grated or cut into tiny pieces. An overdose of cheese, however, will make the sauce stringy. The proper proportions are approximately 1 cup of sauce to ½ cup of cheese. A dash of nutmeg helps.

Almost any of the hard or semihard cheeses—Cheddar, Neufchâtel, Emmentaler, Gruyère, Vermont, New York State, Parmesan—may be employed singly or in combination. Use enough to attain the cheesy flavor sought.

Béchamel is the basic sauce for most soufflés, the best for vegetables or for any other occasion when you require a white or a cheese sauce—most often with liquid-cooked foods or with eggs.

Egg Sauces

There are three great sauces made with eggs: mayonnaise, hollandaise, and *béarnaise*. In each eggs provide some small measure of flavor, but serve principally as part of the emulsion in which the acids—vinegar and/or lemon juice—are blended with oil, butter, or margarine. The egg yolks also act as the thickening agents for these sauces. It is this aspect of their production that seems to frighten off most people. Overcome your fear, and you'll find yourself thinking nothing of stirring up these popular and delicious sauces on your own.

In the company of *sauce vinaigrette* (known in the United States, for reasons inexplicable to me, as Italian or French dressing), mayonnaise is one of the greatest of all cold sauces. It is composed of raw egg, oil, vinegar and/or lemon juice. Hollandaise, a cooked mayonnaise, and its somewhat spicier cousin, *béarnaise*, are the most notable of hot egg sauces. Both mayonnaise and hollandaise form the base for many combination sauces.

Their home production erroneously alarms many normally bold souls. Since I've devoted an entire section of this book to the uses of the egg, I hope by now at least some of the apprehension has been dispelled. These sauces aren't difficult to make.

The first condition you must assume before making either hollandaise or mayonnaise is one of relaxation. Allow yourself all the time you need; don't be hurried. The second is that the eggs and the oil to be used in the preparation be at room temperature. The third has to do with proportions of ingredients.

In the case of mayonnaise, one large egg yolk will blend properly with no more than 4 ounces of olive oil or a quarter pound of butter or margarine. (Margarine makes very good hollandaise and *béarnaise.*)

MAYONNAISE

There are two ways to guarantee the success of your own mayonnaise:
1. Be sure to first add lemon juice and/or vinegar, powdered mustard, salt, white pepper (and sugar if you wish) to the egg yolks. Mix them and allow them to stand for 3 or 4 minutes.
2. Heat the lemon juice or vinegar before pouring it into the yolks, stirring rhythmically as you pour.

I always start to work on mayonnaise with a small wooden spoon. Once under way and ready for the larger quantities of oil, I change over to a wire whisk. The oil should be added almost literally drop by drop at the beginning, and it should be beaten until the shimmer of the oil has completely disappeared from the surface of the mixture. After about a tablespoon of oil has been introduced in this way, you may pour in more oil in larger quantities. The longer you beat it, the thicker the mayonnaise will become. Moreover, if you allow it to rest for an hour or so before you serve it, it will thicken a bit more.

Once the mixing process has been completed, pour in a tablespoon of boiling water and stir it thoroughly, causing the mixture to set. If you find it too bland for your taste, you may add at the very end some more lemon juice and a few grains of cayenne pepper.

Mayonnaise can be made in a blender and only during one period of our lives have I resorted regularly to making it with the aid of a machine, my passion for cooking by hand being what it is. This was while we were living in Ireland, where domestic brands of "salad dressing" were unpalatable and Hellman's obtainable at vast expense. Since both our sons consume mayonnaise in improbable quantities, I reluctantly yielded to my husband's supplications and used the blender, having found the best recipe in the *June Platt Cook Book*. Blender mayonnaise was satisfactory for the boys' gross-feeding purposes, but it lacked the fine flavor and, above all, the texture of the real thing—hand-stirred.

I shan't detain you with a list of all the uses to which mayonnaise can be put. Do, however, remember that it greatly enhances cold vegetables, served individually or as a mixture.

Oil that has been congealed by the cold cannot be used to make mayonnaise. You can detect this condition by noting the presence of particles and of cloudiness. Oil that is too cold won't work either. Place the container in a warm spot until it reaches room temperature.

If some mishap causes the mayonnaise to separate, all is not lost. Start with a new egg yolk and add the curdled sauce to it as if it were the oil in the original process, drop by drop at the start, then in larger quantities.

Remember, courage and "cool" are the best feelings to bring to the making of egg sauces. Try to establish a free and pleasurable rhythm in your beating. While I confess that this isn't essential, it might change your whole outlook with respect to the production of egg sauces. Besides, a steady circular motion, established at your own tempo, can itself be relaxing and therefore pleasant. Above all, don't flail the stuff. This is no occasion for frenzy.

HOLLANDAISE

The greatest hazard to the successful manufacture of hollandaise is too much heat and a hurried approach. If excessive heat is applied, the sauce will curdle; that is, the eggs will solidify, effectively scrambling themselves, separating at the same time from the butter or margarine and acid. For this reason, it is easier to control the heat if you use a double boiler than a *bain-marie* or a substitute—at least until you have become a skilled and casual hand with this sauce.

Mix the yolks and acid (vinegar or lemon juice) with a knob of butter or margarine and place the combination over the simmering water of the double boiler. Then keep adding the butter or margarine bit by bit, cooking the sauce until its consistency is about the same as that of commercial mayonnaise. If you try to make it thicker than this, it may easily curdle. Should the eggs start to scramble all may be saved by adding a little cold cream or canned milk and reducing heat. The minute you have attained the desired thickness, remove it from the top of the double boiler and place it in a gravy boat or serving dish at room temperature. That's all there is to it.

BÉARNAISE

This is a somewhat more savory cousin of hollandaise. You evaporate vinegar with tarragon leaves, shallots, and peppercorns. The residue is pressed through a strainer into the double boiler. Then you proceed as if you were making hollandaise. *Béarnaise* is splendid for service with grilled meats (broiled or panfried) or with fish. I cannot remember a single person to whom I've served *béarnaise* who didn't like it.

One day, when I was reading a cookbook (a habit I'll never be able to break), I came upon mention of *sauce paloise*. "*Palois*" is the adjective applied to the city of Pau, in southwestern France, where we've spent two summers. I had never, during our stays there, been served this sauce or heard it mentioned. I turned to the recipe and realized at once that in reality it was a *sauce béarnaise* (Pau is the capital of the old province of Béarn) in which the tarragon had been replaced by mint. I tried to imagine how this creation came into being, and conjured up an explanation that may or may not be the right one.

Pau was for many decades an autumnal resort for the horse-loving British. It is set in fine hunting country. It seems obvious to me that an English gentleman, upon being served a roast of lamb, demanded mint sauce. The chef thus importuned had to improvise, never having heard of English mint sauce or mint jelly. *Sauce paloise* is the tasty result. That's my story, at any rate, and I'm sticking to it until I hear a better one.

Tomato Sauce

The reference here *isn't* to the kind of tomato sauce you serve with Italian dishes. This is the variety you would add to the dish itself or use in combination with other sauces. You would also choose it when you are seeking a flavor less robust and less rich than the classic Italian sauce. It may be used with anything you believe might be improved by the addition of a good tomato sauce: meat, fish, vegetables, and eggs; your imagination is the only barrier.

Before you have anything to do with tomatoes, you must begin with butter, in which you sauté diced onions, salt pork, and carrots. The process should continue until the onions have "melted." That is, until they have become clear. When the vegetables are tender, add flour to them and make a *roux*. Cook this combination until it begins to brown.

The liquid vehicle for tomato sauce is white stock. Fish stock is ideal if you mean to use it with seafood. As usual, the stock should be heated before it is added to the *roux*. This is also the moment when the tomatoes are added. They should represent about twice the volume of the sauce so far produced. Ideally, they will be fresh and ripe, seeded and peeled, or they may be canned. Introduce as well some crushed garlic, pepper, a pinch of sugar, some thyme and bay leaf. This mixture must cook for at least 90 minutes (either simmered on top of the stove, or in a covered container in the oven). Then it should be strained (to trap the elusive tomato seeds) and brought to a boil once more, stirring thoroughly to bring it all together after the straining has been completed. Canned tomato paste is an adequate substitute, but those who have the time will go the extra mile to use fresh tomatoes. This sauce, incidentally, keeps well in the refrigerator.

Sauce Vinaigrette (*alias Italian or French Dressing*)
The simplest and often the best dressing for salads and cold dishes is *sauce vinaigrette* made of oil, vinegar, salt, pepper, and sometimes dry or prepared mustard. Most recipes call for 3 parts of oil to 1 of vinegar.

Why is it that most *sauces vinaigrettes* taste too harsh and strong? It has taken me many years to make a discovery I now pass on: Most of the cheaper varieties of domestic vinegar have a much higher degree of acidity than do the imported and finer domestic kinds. Therefore, you must either dilute your vinegar with wine or use different proportions from those usually recommended—4 parts of oil to each of vinegar instead of the prescribed 3.

Vinaigrette and the sauces that derive from it are splendid with cold vegetables and cold meats, even with cold starches, like marrow beans.

COMPOUND SAUCES

I feel more or less secure in stating categorically that all sauces other than those I've discussed so far are combinations of two or more of them, though some are made by the addition of ingredients—like introducing peppers to the tomato sauce or cheese to the white sauce.

As you will have perhaps noted, the relationship of the basic sauces to the compound ones is very like that of the simple to the combination cooking processes. The most constructive advice I can offer is that you embark on the production of compound sauces with respect—that you not waste the elements of the basic sauces by adding to them ingredients that won't blend properly. Proceed with caution. Thus your course should be without serious peril.

Throughout this chapter I have stressed the need to allow plenty of time in the preparation of sauces, whether homogeneous or contrasting. However, from time to time we have all been caught short and had to rush the making of a sauce. This shouldn't occur. If you have an hour and a half in which to prepare a meal, you can make a basic or a compound sauce to serve with it by starting it first, then proceeding to the other elements of the dinner. It's just a question of good planning.

Sauce Espagnole

Although it is not the purpose of this book to furnish recipes, I think it might be useful to offer an example of sauce cooking by citing a single recipe, for *sauce espagnole*, to demonstrate the preparation of a compound sauce. As a matter of fact, some other sauces are *based on sauce espagnole*. These may seem difficult to make, and they certainly demand thought and time, but the difficulties vanish once you understand they are combinations of the basic sauces and techniques, employed in a further building process.

Sauce Espagnole

INGREDIENTS

½ cup fat (drippings saved from beef, bacon, stock, duck, turkey, etc.)
½ cup flour
8 cups brown stock (or equivalent quantity of beef bouillon or cubes)
1 tablespoon thyme
½ cup tomato sauce (or 3 tablespoons tomato paste)
Salt and pepper

PROCEDURE

Melt the fat in a 3-quart saucepan.

Blend in the flour and cook until the color of the mixture is like that of hazelnuts. (To you, if you have been following the various steps described in this and earlier chapters, this means: Make a brown *roux*, using ½ cup flour and ½ cup fat.)

Add 6 cups of stock. Stir well and allow to simmer for 4 hours. (Liquefy the *roux*.)

Add thyme, tomato (sauce or paste), and the remaining 2 cups of stock. Simmer for 2 more hours.

Strain, then flavor with salt and pepper.

Note that this sauce keeps well in the refrigerator and can even be frozen. It comes in handy for use as it is, or for making an even more complicated sauce, like *bordelaise*.

But just imagine how difficult the recipe for *sauce espagnole* would seem if none of the cooking "shorthand" was employed—if every single step had to be described in detail in every recipe. We would all probably stop cooking, or certainly would avoid attempts to make some of these superb sauces. However, by mastering the basic principles, these marvels are accessible to you—always assuming that you have planned ahead, making good use of time and the refrigerator, so that you are never called on to make a compound sauce in a single, continuous operation.

10

Punctuation: *Herbs and Spices, Salts, Sweeteners*

"The Hidden Soul" Maître Escoffier quotes Grinod de la Reynière, another great French cook, as observing that aromatics are "the hidden soul of cooking," and indeed they are the highlighters, the qualifiers and modifiers of a kitchen grammar. These are the topic of this chapter—herbs, spices, salts, sugars, and their kind, which are used to enhance and flatter the essential flavor of a dish, but never to disguise it. As all dieters can assure you, the addition of herbs and spices may help to make it possible for one to remain on a diet without suffering what amounts to cruel and unusual punishment attributable to a surfeit of blandness.

Especially in the days before refrigeration in hot, and even in temperate, climates, some spices were often deployed to make palatable products that had become putrid. In fact, there are some food neurotics who still imagine this to be the case, who are convinced that a well-flavored dish is somehow poisonous. This is a ridiculous misconception of the role of these products.

An oyster with a squeeze of lemon juice, or a boiled new potato with freshly chopped parsley, a dash of paprika on a scrambled egg—all basic ingredients are enhanced by the flavorings added to them. Part of the idea of this chapter is the marriage of flavorings. We use the word "marry" in its ideal sense when applying it to cooking: a combination that makes the whole greater than its component parts. In cooking, it way well be an open marriage, since often more than two ingredients are combined for this end.

Train Yourself to Think About Flavors

For the proper use of highlighters, you have to train yourself to think as you taste. This isn't so difficult as it may seem, because you already know what you are supposed to be thinking about. Naturally, you must first familiarize yourself with the flavors of the numerous highlighting products that are available to you, so you can know how they taste and which to use in what combinations. Most spice jars give some hints about their application, and so do the recipes you'll be following, so you needn't feel you are starting out in total darkness.

This is not at all like the wine-tasting game. It is not as if someone were to produce a sauce, for example, and ask you what it is composed of—a trying and testing sport which many of the world's best cooks can't successfully participate in, nor do they feel the need to meet such a challenge. Cooking of superior quality has nothing whatever to do with gamesmanship.

The reason thinking about flavors is important to cooking is that there is simply no way that I or anyone else can state flatly that a tablespoon of a dried or fresh herb or spice will taste to *you* in a precisely definable fashion. We can't even do it for ourselves. The quality of the products and the conditions under which they have been grown and processed, even their age and the sort of storage to which they have been subjected, are factors which may, for instance, affect the amount of oil they retain and their strength. I can't state as a certainty that one brand of herbs and spices is more reliable than any other all the time, or that home-grown varieties will invariably be preferable to those you buy in a market, because there are too many unknowns.

It is generally true, I think, that herbs produced in the Mediterranean basin (like sage, thyme, and rosemary) are the best; they are grown in poor soil, without excessive rainfall, but in lots of sunlight, those being the conditions that result in the creation of the most oil in a plant. I don't know why French-grown tarragon is better than Russian, but it is.

As a cook, *you* have to discover how, through the experience of actually adding spices and herbs bit by bit, you arrive at exactly the flavor that suits your taste. It *is* possible to state with total confidence that too much of any herb or spice is bad, very bad. Don't ever forget this. Consequently, it is important to bear constantly in mind that while you can add these flavorings if you find a dish too bland, you can't eliminate them if you have overdone it. Only the novice cook believes that a dish too redolent of a particular flavor is good.

As a rule, the portion of an herb plant used for flavoring is the leaf; in some instances the seed. The flower, bark, root, or seed may contain the essence of a spice.

Certain seasonings are absolute necessities for every kitchen. Others will be required if you plan to make particular foreign specialties—those dependent on the nation whose cooking you happen to favor.

BASIC HERBS

Here is a list of basic herbs and a list of spices that you should always have on hand. Once you have mastered their use, you ought to begin experimenting with others that are a bit more recondite.

Basic Herbs 145

BASIL (leaf): Sweet, fragrant. The perfect herb for tomatoes. A must in Italian cooking. For flavoring vinegars.

BAY (leaf), also called laurel. Strong and pungent. For meats, poultry, fish, stews, and soups. One of the most important ingredients in a *bouquet garni*. To be used with caution.

CHERVIL (leaf): Mild and aromatic. Best when fresh. Lovely leaf. May be used in lieu of parsley. Great with mushrooms.

CHIVES (the mildest of the onion family): For garnish, soups, cottage cheese, baked potatoes, cold dishes, eggs.

DILL: Fragrant, haunting flavor. Leaf is used for soups, potatoes, eggs, cottage cheese, seafood (especially shrimp), vinegar, and pickles; seed is used to flavor pickles, fish stuffing, and vinegars.

FENNEL: A mild, fragrant, licorice flavor. Leaf is used for sauces, cold dishes, Italian food. Seed for cakes and stuffings. Bulb and stalks are used as vegetables and in salads. It is now stylish to roast fish on fennel twigs.

GARLIC: Very strong, pungent, the most powerful of the onion family. Use with great discretion. Sections called "cloves" are used in crushed or chopped form for meats, fish, sauces, poultry, vegetables, salads, and for flavoring vinegar.

JUNIPER (berry): Pungent, the essential flavor of gin. Use in *pâtés*, sauerkraut, game, and pork. Middle European, German, and Dutch cooking, particularly.

MARJORAM (leaf): Very strong flavor, close to that of oregano. For soups, sauces, meat dishes, and fish stuffing.

MINT (leaf): Mild, fresh taste. For tea, lamb, vinegar, peas, soups, jellies, fruits, sauces.

OREGANO (leaf): Pungent (see marjoram). The essential herb in Italian cooking. May be used when you seek a flavor stronger than that of thyme.

PARSLEY (leaf and thin part of stem): Mild, enhancing flavor. For *bouquet garni*, decoration, and for use with any vegetable, meat, poultry, or eggs.

ROSEMARY (leaf): Strong and pungent. For lamb, pork, mutton, goose, sauces, sausages, and soups.

SAGE (leaf): Very strong. Use with caution. For poultry, sausages, and stuffings.

TARRAGON (leaf): A lively fragrance, mild licorice aura—the monarch of herbs. For soups, sauces, flavoring of butter, poultry, vinegar, and the decoration of cold dishes.
THYME (leaf): Pungent and fragrant. Indispensable for stews, soups, many sauces, sausage stuffing, *bouquet garni.*

Bouquet Garni

The accepted formula for a *bouquet garni* is parsley, thyme, and bay leaf, tied together (or wrapped in cheesecloth) for easy removal from the pot in which it has been placed. When introduced in powdered form, you don't need to worry about removing it. You may want to add carrots and leeks to your *bouquet garni,* something I frequently do. Celery leaves and stalks are considered indispensable by some; garlic is also used sometimes.

Fines Herbes

This is a mixture of 2 parts chive, 1 part chervil, and 1 part tarragon. As a matter of personal taste, I add 1 part dill. The flavor of this combination is sublime.

BASIC SPICES

ALLSPICE (berry): Flavor like a mixture of cinnamon, clove, and nutmeg. Used whole or ground for meats, gravies, *pâtés,* sausages, curry powder, cakes, pies, and meat loaf.
CAYENNE (pod or powder): *Very* hot pepper. For cream sauces, pickles, or any dish requiring the hottest of the peppery seasonings.
CINNAMON (bark): Pungent, distinctive flavor and aroma. For beverages, meats, breads, pastries, fruits, and preserves.
CLOVES (dried buds): Pungent flavor and scent, high oil content. For meats, vegetables, preserves, pickles, marinades, fruit desserts, and toothaches. Often used with onion in stock.
GINGER (root): Very fragrant and pungent. Young roots are candied as a confection and made into preserves. Older roots are dried and ground for use in gingerbread, meats, desserts, sausages, *pâtés,* cakes, and curries.

MACE (outer shell of nutmeg): Flavor is a cross between nutmeg and cinnamon. For cream sauces, sweet pastries and cookies, cheese dishes, soups, meats, fish, shellfish, and vegetables.

MUSTARD (leaves and seeds, prepared and powdered): Young leaves may be served as a vegetable or in a salad. Powdered, it is used in sauces, salad dressings, meats, eggs, poultry, and pickles. Prepared mustard may be used alone or in some meat sauces.

All nations have their types of prepared mustard. In cooking generally, the powdered English and the mixed Dijon French varieties are best because of their purity of flavor.

NUTMEG (packaged whole or powdered): Whole is best, so that you can grate it when you need it. This is the nut of the nutmeg tree. For cakes, fruits, vegetables, meats, sauces, soups, and milk drinks.

PAPRIKA (mild pepper, usually available only in powdered form): Pungent. Hungarian and Spanish varieties available. For Hungarian cooking, seasoning, decoration for fish, cheese, meats, salads, vegetables, and eggs.

BLACK AND WHITE PEPPER (whole or ground berries or "corns"): White pepper is actually black pepper with the husk rubbed off. White is slightly milder. It is preferable to buy the corns whole and grind them as needed. Both are used in all aspects of cooking except in sweets. Peppercorns are used whole in stews, soups, and sausages.

SAFFRON (dried stamen of a Spanish crocus): Whole or powdered. Adds lovely yellow coloring. Pungent and aromatic. Use with discretion. For soups, sauces, cakes, rice dishes, preserves, curries, and *bouillabaisse*.

VANILLA (pod of an orchid): Available whole or in an extract (with alcohol base). If you keep a vanilla bean in a supply of sugar, the sugar will be perfectly flavored for desserts. The bean form is superior to the extract. Avoid the "simulated" type. For pastries, custards, chocolate, sweet sauces, ice cream. If you insert the bean in milk when heating for a sweet sauce, it will impart its flavor. Dry it after used, and you can use it again.

ZEST OF ORANGE OR LEMON: The oils from the skins of these

fruits may be used by rubbing them on lumps of sugar to impregnate the cubes with flavor. Also, thin slices may be kept in a sugar supply to impart their flavor, as does the vanilla bean. Thinly sliced rinds for use in sauces and marinades. Blends well with bitter chocolate. A must for making authentic *crêpes Suzette*. You can also dry thin strips to have on hand.

Quatre Épices

You'll find the need for *quatre épices* (or Parisian spice) mainly in French recipes. In France, it comes already packaged. You may satisfactorily substitute allspice for *quatre épices*. However, if you want to make the real thing, here are the ingredients: 1 part cayenne, 3 parts thyme, 3 parts ginger, 3 parts mace, 4 parts clove, 4 parts cinnamon, 6 parts nutmeg, 5 parts ground white pepper, 5 parts ground black pepper, and 5 parts ground bay leaf. You don't have to be much of a mathematician to observe that *"quatre" épices* combines, in fact, ten different elements. When I'm making my own, I use for measurement a "pinch," or occasionally a small mustard spoon. The quantities need not be precise. However, nothing affords the "Cordon Bleu" touch of professional excellence to a *pâté* or even a humble pot roast so well as a small quantity of this exotic mixture. It need not be prepared just prior to use. As a matter of fact, you should prepare a fair-sized batch, mix it with an equal portion of kosher salt, and store it almost indefinitely in a tight-lidded jar or metal box.

SALTS

It may come as something of a surprise to discover that there is more to salt than the simple chemical sodium chloride. Perhaps it is the most important of all the highlighters. Just imagine food without it.

There is a surprising variety. Sea salt is evaporated from sea water. Caution! Sea salt is much "saltier" than any other variety. Rock salt is quarried and broken into pebbles or granulated, so that it pours when it rains. I suggest that in most instances you avoid regular "table" salt in favor of kosher salt, whose flavor I can only describe as "fresher," though I can't say why this should be so. Perhaps it is because the crystals are larger. When you try it, you'll remark on the difference at once.

In addition to its use as a flavoring, of course, salt is a significant preserving agent, used in pickling and curing.

Monosodium Glutamate

Under several different names (including its initials, M.S.G.), this chemical, originating with Chinese cooking, has gained general acceptance as a tenderizer and flavor enhancer. My own reaction is that it is fine in its primordial application. Note that its habitual use is of doubtful advisability from a medical point of view—but this is true of so many pleasant things we eat that I advance the counsel without great conviction.

ACIDS: VINEGARS

The basic cooking acid is, of course, vinegar. But, as with salt, there are numerous types: cider, red and white wine, and vinegars that have been flavored with different herbs.

Lemon or, less frequently, orange juice may be employed in certain cases, even in the making of *sauce vinaigrette* and marinades.

HOT SEASONINGS

Varieties of pepper are corns (white and black), paprika, chili, cayenne, bell, and mixed peppers. They give spectacular vitality to certain dishes—steak au poivre, for instance —or in the curing of ham. Curry powder is an exotic mixture of many herbs, spices, and peppers used as a flavoring and to make a sauce.

PUNGENTS

The pungents consist primarily of chives, shallots, scallions, onions, garlic, and horseradish—they are the great donors of "personality" to cooking.

HOT CONDIMENTS

These are mustards, pickles (especially sweet and sour gherkins), capers, and a host of spicy sauces of varying degrees of savor and heat, prepared by food packagers or of your own devising. For use by themselves or as contributions to saucemaking.

SWEETENERS

Sweeteners are basically honey and sugar. But, as we are familiar with the different sorts of sugar, so are there different types of honey that are worth becoming acquainted with—from the very dark Greek variety to the ubiquitous clover honey. Sugars range from the darkest brown crystals to granulated white and confectioner's sugar. Then, too, as noted above, you may flavor your sugar with such additives as vanilla beans, citrus peels, and cinnamon.

It seems superfluous to describe the uses of sweeteners. They sweeten.

As you become accustomed to using them, herbs and spices will come to seem increasingly indispensable to your cooking. You'll doubtless discover some favorites. But a final caution: Like a favorite color, a favorite flavor can be a pleasure to you and a bore to others. Be discreet. Be various. Be venturesome—and be cautious. Spice is the variety of cooking life.

11

The Complementary Phrase: *Baking*

The Mystery of Touch in Pastry

I think most people intimately connected with the preparation of food would agree (after an argument, of course) that there are two kinds of cooks: regular cooks and pastry cooks. In France and in the rest of Europe, the two crafts are recognized as separate culinary disciplines, two distinct aspects of foodmaking. Of the two, I believe it is easier to become a great regular cook than a great pastry cook. I know that it is not altogether helpful to volunteer the opinion that in both instances a mystique is involved. I think this is the case and need not defend the position, since a mystique is an article of faith and thus defies reason.

I have an example of what I mean in my own household. My daughter Susan is a born pastry cook. Now twenty-two, she has been cooking since she was eight. But from her first pie crust (made slightly gray by the dirt imbedded beneath her fingernails), there was no escaping the conclusion that she had the true baker's touch. She uses *my* recipes. *I* was her teacher. Now she's my master. However, I'm bound to observe that there are some things I can teach without being able to learn them myself—qualities that are purely instinctive or intuitive: a mystique.

If someone were to tell me that I had only one more dish to prepare in my life, I'd respond with a main course and a sauce suitable for consumption by the most important of angels. I needn't ask Susan what she'd make; it would be a magnificent piece of pastry.

A *Little History*

The piemaking and cakemaking tradition is ancient in the United States and Great Britain. Women who wouldn't deign to sully their hands in the kitchen under normal circumstances to make, for instance, a stew, would devote their energies tirelessly to the preparation of a special cake. The continental European tradition is quite different, however. There it is the custom to purchase tarts and cakes in fine pastry shops. I wholly approve of this practice and would follow it myself if there were satisfactory *pâtisseries* in my neighborhood. Given the choice of preparing a good meal —that is, a repast of appetizer, fish and/or meat course, and salad—or a dessert, the European cook will almost invariably consider it her principal obligation to compose the body of the meal and resort to the purchase of the dessert, since pastries and other confections are considered better done by professionals.

Many of us in the New World follow the British tradition —a tradition, I feel constrained to point out, not renowned for its fine cuisine. We spend a whole day baking, leaving the main portion of the meal as something of a stepchild, to be prepared haphazardly at the last minute. Lack of demand for superb pastry shops has imposed on us, whether we like it or not, the necessity for some baking.

A Family Story

A note of some antiquity: My great-grandmother was Viennese. Her husband was a Danish *bon vivant* in the great European manner of the nineteenth century—certainly the golden age of great cooking. He cared so much about food that each spring found him in Paris for the first of the asparagus. Their home was in Philadelphia, where there was no bakery capable of producing a *Dobosch Torte*. Consequently, my great-grandmother confected one of these incredibly rich pastries every Saturday morning, using the dining room table as her working surface. The maid would bring in the ingredients and the lady of the house would put them together. I'm sorry that that hideous golden-oak table, with its mature-breasted, griffon-shaped legs, has disappeared from the family. The image of that ritual, often described to me, is one that I shall always cherish.

The making of bread, I feel, has no proper place in this book. If you are one of the many who feel a need to manufacture bread because of its historical or sociological implications, you should acquire one of the excellent volumes devoted exclusively to the subject, for it is very extensive. The selection of such a book should be made with the advice of a friend who is a knowledgeable baker. I am not one. Julia Child and Simone Beck, in the second volume of *Mastering the Art of French Cooking*, satisfy my own needs.

BAKING CAKES

Louis P. de Gouy (that really was his name—"Gouy" pronounced like the French "Louis"—and he was J. P. Morgan's personal chef) dedicated pages of his excellent work, *The Gold Cook Book*, to the causes of and remedies for mistakes made in the baking of cakes. I won't attempt here to recapitulate any of the exhaustive detail he furnishes so well—such as his disquisition on the tendency of flour to retain moisture and its effect on a cake. Since I believe I'm writing mainly for the beginning cook, I urge you to consult de Gouy for greater expertise. My desire here is to suggest approaches to the preparation of cakes that will bring you to the procedure in a relaxed and eager frame of mind—the main accomplishment I was able to transmit to my daughter.

Ingredients

All the ingredients for home baking ought to be of the very best.

I use unbleached flour unless the recipe specifically calls for cake flour. Self-rising flours are to be avoided if not suggested.

Use large eggs unless otherwise noted. (Some recipes give egg quantities by volume rather than by numbers of eggs because of size variants.)

I always use sweet (unsalted) butter. For one thing, I can be more certain of its freshness. It is possible to use margarine or hydrogenated fat, but the resulting pastry won't have the fine flavor that is imparted by sweet butter.

The best milk is also a necessity.

All of the ingredients for cakemaking should be at room temperature when you are ready to use them. For practical purposes, "room temperature" is between 68° and 75°.

Sugar is available in so many varieties that some qualification is in order. Certain cooks recommend the use of superfine sugar instead of the normal granulated kind. You may also use vanilla-flavored sugar (see p. 147 for a description of its preparation). If you have none of this on hand, use pure vanilla—never the artificial variety. This injunction about the "genuine" article applies to any other flavoring you need. It is almost invariably a false economy, at least in terms of taste.

Most cake recipes call for cream of tartar, bicarbonate of soda (the same as the bathroom staple), or a double-acting baking powder. Be certain to have a supply of the type specified.

Equipment
    3 bowls for breaking eggs (see p. 103)
    Mixing bowl
    Baking pans
    Flour sifter
    Measuring spoons
    Measuring cups
    Egg beater or electric mixer
    Cake tester or a clean piece of straw
    Chopping bowl and chopper, or grater, for nuts
    Pot for melting chocolate or other special flavoring
    Cake racks
    Cooling racks
    Waxed paper
    Whatever other special utensils required for the particular recipe

Techniques of Cake Baking
Place the oven rack in the middle position. Unless otherwise stipulated, all baking is done at this level in the oven.

As a rule, set the oven temperature at 350°–375°, unless a different heat is called for. As I've observed in an earlier chapter, it is important to know the idiosyncracies of your oven.

Butter your baking pans thoroughly but thinly; what you seek is a fine film of butter. Excessive buttering will cause your crust to be heavy. Sometimes a recipe suggests that you line the pans with waxed paper; follow this advice.

Flour the pans by swirling a tablespoon of flour around the inside of the utensils until the film of butter has been completely coated. Empty the residue from the pans by giving them a firm tap on the edge of your sink.

Separate the eggs in the manner described on p. 103.

Tear off two handy-sized pieces of waxed paper and place them on your working surface—counter or tabletop.

Measure and sift the flour and any other dry ingredients onto one of the pieces of waxed paper. The paper can subsequently assist you in pouring the flour, etc., into another receptable and then be thrown away. Place your sifted flour on the piece of waxed paper, so you waste none of the measured portions.

After accurately measuring the amounts of butter and sugar required, cream them until the mixture is white but not runny. The object is *not* to cause the butter to melt. For this operation you can use a wooden spoon, your bare hands, or an electric mixer.

Beat the egg yolks until they are thick and lemon yellow in color.

If you have only one egg beater, wash it and dry it thoroughly to have it ready for use when you need it to beat the whites. Remember that the presence of any oil residue on the beater or in the bowl will adversely affect the egg whites.

Mix the ingredients in accordance with the instructions of the recipe you have chosen.

Beat the egg whites until they are stiff but still glistening.

Mix a small amount of the whites into the dough. Then fold the remainder of the whites in with the dough.

Divide the dough equally into the requisite number of baking pans.

Place the pans in the oven. Be sure to allow about 2 inches between the pans and a comparable amount of space between each pan and the four sides of the oven.

Do *not* open the oven door until 10 minutes before the baking time should be completed. Test and watch the remainder of the baking with care, for you don't want to overbake your cake.

The cake is done when the tester emerges from it absolutely clean.

Unless the directions tell you differently, let it cool for about 20 minutes.

Run a dull knife around the circumference of the pan to loosen the cake.

With the assistance of a cool damp cloth applied to the bottom of the pan, turn the cake out on a rack to cool completely before icing it.

Such are the general directions for the baking of a cake. If, however, they differ in any respect from the recipe you are following, *by all means adhere to the directions of the recipe to the very letter.*

Most cakes are merely enriched forms of bread that have soda rather than yeast as the leavening agent. They are also leavened and bound with eggs and should be light and of a uniform texture throughout.

A Bouncing Birthday Cake

Having offered such elaborate directions, I feel honor bound to confess to my greatest cooking failure. I had promised my sister Jo that I would bake the cake for her twenty-first birthday party. The recipe I selected was for a sponge cake, for I was entranced with the idea of an icing and frosting of mocha and butter cream (half chocolate, half coffee flavored), with an almond praline dusted over the top.

I made the cake, put it into the oven, and then directed my attention to the part of the process that really intrigued me—the praline, which was caramelized almonds (in a slightly burned mixture of sugar and water). I broke the nuts into small pieces and ground them up, then mixed them with the mocha cream. I tasted the combination. God, but it was good! I removed the cake from the oven, applied the frosting and then decided that it would be best if it were served cold, so I placed it in the refrigerator. I was delighted with myself.

When the moment arrived for my sister to cut the cake, she applied a knife and discovered with the initial stroke of the blade that she was making no appreciable incision. It refused to yield. It was like rubber. The explanation, of course, was that I'd failed to allow the cake to cool before applying the frosting, and then compounded that felony by refrigerating it at once, thus sealing in all the vapors. It was spongy in more ways than one. I don't think Jo ever quite forgave me.

PREPARING PASTRY

Pastry is a combination of flour, salt, fat, and sometimes sugar, as closely wedded as possible, blended with egg, ice water, or even cream cheese as the binder.

There are many pastry recipes for different purposes. You don't, for instance, use the same formula for a meat pie that you use for an apple pie or a strawberry tart. Choose the pastry best suited to the purpose you intend. For meat pies, to cite an example, I use one in which lard and butter are employed.

No matter what the particular ingredients for making a pastry, the process is fundamentally the same for all. As distinct from the making of cakes, you should work pastry ingredients at as cool a temperature as you can manage. You should also avoid laboring it, i.e., mixing it longer than it takes to make the ingredients just blend.

Equipment
Measuring cup
Two sheets of waxed paper
Large plate or platter
Fork
Knife or pastry blender
Bowl for ice water or egg
Sifter
Pie pan
Rolling pin
A dull knife

As with cakemaking, you should use only the finest basic ingredients for pastry. Margarine may be substituted for sweet butter.

Techniques of Pastrymaking
Sift flour and salt three times.

While the fat is still firm, dice it into pieces the size of peas and bury these nuggets in the flour.

With a knife, a fork, or a pastry blender (I recommend the last), cut into the flour-and-fat mixture until its consistency is that of cornmeal.

If you prefer to mix your pastry with your fingers (my daughter does), take pinches of flour and fat in both hands and gently rub them between your thumbs and first two fingers. When these bits become grainy, repeat the procedure with more flour and fat until the entire quantity has the texture of cornmeal. The process will be easier if you cut the pieces of fat into tiny bits, burying them in the flour at the beginning.

Bind with water and/or egg (or whatever else your recipe proposes as a proper binder).

Wrap in foil or waxed paper and allow it to rest in the refrigerator for at least 2 hours. A full 24-hour period is preferable. (A recent experience jarred me. On a visit to a family camp in the Adirondacks, we were served an apple pie with a perfect crust. On complimenting the chef, I learned that he had stored *his* pastry in the refrigerator for two weeks!)

When you remove the ball of dough from the refrigerator, warm it in the palms of your hands.

Roll it out on a smooth, flour-covered surface with a rolling pin. The rolling pin should also be covered with flour, otherwise it will stick to the dough. With fragile dough, rolling between sheets of waxed paper or using a pastry cloth and roller cover will facilitate the almost impossible operation.

To move the thin layer of dough, roll it very loosely on the rolling pin and then unroll it over the pie pan or dish.

Puff Pastry

I strongly suggest that you not attempt to make a puff pastry until you are absolutely sure of your touch with ordinary pastry dough. When you have reached that point, all you need do (as with cakemaking) is to follow closely the recipe you find the easiest to understand.

MAKING COOKIES

When you are studying recipes for cookies, try to determine whether the dough described resembles more closely that for cake or pastry. This will furnish the clue as to how you should proceed. Then all you have to do is follow the directions for making either the batter or dough. "Batter," by the way, like so many English cooking terms, comes from the French word for beating, *"battre."*

I have two thoughts by way of conclusion for this chapter. The first is a restatement of what I noted at the outset. Great bakers, like good spellers, are born, not made. The second is quite different: If you enjoy baking, it is really a lot more interesting (and therefore more rewarding) to start with "original" ingredients, not the cake and pie mixes that are both expensive and often not nearly so satisfactory. To have the pride of accomplishing the whole thing from scratch is important—a kind of ego trip.

12

The Indispensable Predicate: *Vegetables, Starches, and Fruits*

Popeye and I   One of my earliest memories associated with food concerns a vegetable. In the late twenties or early thirties, before Philadelphia's Penn Athletic Club ceased to exist, my father was a member in order that he might play handball. Whenever my mother took me to the city, we would lunch at the club because they served what was then my favorite away-from-home dish. A trip to Philadelphia would have been incomplete (regardless of Mother's distaste for the club) if I were deprived of the creamed spinach served there. I recall only vague details of the dining room's furnishings, but I remember vividly three other things about the Penn Athletic Club: climbing into a high chair; the stares of others eating when I called out in my crowlike voice, "Creamed spinach, please"; and the flavor of the dish when presented—which was perfection.

VEGETABLES

If you want perfect vegetables for your table, you have to grow your own, treating the soil with respect, adding the proper fertilizers, using the finest seeds, and cultivating or mulching the garden with care. Then, when the vegetables are ripening, you must pick each one when it is just *au point*, then rush it to stove and table. Naturally, you'll have selected the seed for the strain that produces the product best suited to your need—for immediate consumption or for preservation by canning or freezing—and you'll have followed all the directions noted above.

However, there are comparatively few of us, no matter how deeply we care about the quality of the vegetables we serve, who *do* grow our own. Since this is the case, we must reconcile ourselves to the fact that our "best" in vegetables and other produce is a compromise with perfection. Of course, if you are fortunate enough to go to the country for the summer, it is possible to find good vegetables that have been picked at the instant of their prime and brought directly from the patch to a reliable roadside stand. But this is not a source on which you can count throughout the year.

What I have written about meats holds true for vegetables as well. You'll often find superior fresh produce in city markets that cater to ethnic groups who demand the best—serious, dedicated cooks. Where neither of these conditions prevails, my advice is to sample the various brands of frozen vegetables and, when you find the ones you like best, stock up on them to the extent that your freezer's capacity allows. It is not necessarily true that the same packer invariably produces the best quality of each product, so you shouldn't become a slave to a particular brand.

Over the screams of some purists who'll accuse me of heresy, the point I'm trying to make about vegetables is that the frozen varieties (and some can't be frozen at all) come nearest to the prescription I have outlined above. So if you are unable to find produce that you are certain has been properly grown and freshly picked, you'll be much better off with the frozen.

There are some kinds of vegetables—the ones that are called "semiperishable"—that stand up fairly well to the rigors of shipping and storage, like the roots: potatoes, beets, onions, carrots, etc. And certain other fresh produce—broccoli, squash, peppers, and cauliflower—also survive storage well and are often good buys in supermarkets. Some vegetables, like green beans, fall into a category that is marginal—to be bought fresh only if the quality and the price are right. It would be absurd, in terms of both expense and taste, to buy these in frozen form, unless you live in an area where no satisfactory fresh produce at all is available.

Given my support of frozen vegetables, it may seem both perverse and old-fashioned of me to express the conviction that some varieties—especially sweet corn—should be served as a separate dish *only* when the local article is in season. My late friend, the great gourmet-journalist A. J. Liebling, once compared the perishability of sweet corn with the flavor of southern politics, observing that both lost something for every hundred yards they traveled from the patch where they were grown. Amen!

Of course, this prohibition doesn't apply to the use of frozen or canned corn in a recipe. But, like pornography, excessive exposure to a seasonable vegetable or fruit detracts from the excitement and anticipation of consuming it. Other examples of this are asparagus and berries—which I refuse to serve out of season. But when the strawberry or asparagus periods are in full swing, we have real orgies of them. We have a meal that consists solely of southern-style strawberry shortcake made with heavy biscuit dough, lavished with crushed, sweetened berries and unsweetened whipped cream. The slightly salty biscuit is covered with butter, then the berries and whipped cream are added. It is a true strawberry festival, a pleasure worth waiting a whole year for.

An Exceptional Can

Some canned vegetables shouldn't be disdained—beets and baby carrots, for instance. Certain canned "dried" beans are also acceptable, though much more expensive than preparing your own from packets. Some cooks relish the different flavor that the canning process imparts, for example, to peas and asparagus. When I'm in Europe, I often purchase canned *macédoine* of vegetables. I find that I can make of that mixture very fine *oeufs à la russe*, with the addition of finely grated onion, fresh parsley, and homemade mayonnaise. On the other hand, the cook who buys canned onions or potatoes shouldn't bother reading this book.

Obviously, there are many dishes, no matter what the season, that call for the use of canned vegetables and pastes. In both instances, I strongly recommend purchasing the imported varieties whenever possible. If you have to pinch pennies, I suggest—as an example—that you buy imported whole tomatoes and domestic tomato paste, adding to the latter your own seasoning of fresh or dried basil.

Living Near Gardens

I appreciate the fact that for some readers who have the good fortune to live near one of the great garden market areas, most of what I've written about vegetables isn't necessarily applicable. One of my sisters, who lives in Oregon, makes my Upstate New York soul turn a shade of envious green when she describes the plethora of vegetables obtainable in Portland all the year-round: three or four varieties of carrot, four different kinds of potato, a myriad of lettuces to choose from, and so on. It is when such images come to mind that one realizes that most big produce shippers find it financially uninteresting to traffic in anything that requires care. And then I find myself echoing my reactionary acquaintances who say, "Nobody gives a damn anymore." Of course, which Americans *ever* gave a damn about food before the end of World War II?

Judging Fresh Vegetables

In no matter what season, there are some tests that you can apply to determine the quality of produce. Unless a bean, a lima bean, or an asparagus stalk snaps when you bend it, don't buy it. If a peapod doesn't pop when you squeeze it, pass it by. If the bottom of an artichoke stem doesn't turn white when you scratch it, avoid it. A cabbage is worthless (and tasteless) if it's not firm and if the colors of its leaves aren't white and green. If a bunch of celery or a leafy vegetable is limp or has many brown leaves, it's not for you. Sprouting onions or potatoes should be eschewed, as should vegetables that have developed wrinkles or faded leaves. The expense of all produce, whether it is fresh or processed, is so great today that it really doesn't make sense to buy anything less than the best available. Not only do you offend your palate, but the amount of waste almost always makes a "bargain" an extravagance.

Preparing Fresh Vegetables

All fresh vegetables should be washed in water whose temperature is lukewarm to warm. We know that cold water doesn't clean our hands. Why should we imagine that it cleans vegetables? Afterward, they can be soaked in cold water.

Peel or shell the vegetable as near as possible to the time you are planning to cook it. If you are putting vegetables into a stew, for instance, start by peeling those that require the longest time to cook; in other words, peel in order of pot priority. Avoid leaving peeled vegetables for long periods in cold water; both flavor and minerals soak away. Be sure to replace your peeler when it gets dull, for a sharp one saves time and does a more effective job. (I suppose some husbands can sharpen them. Mine can't.) For the same reason, all graters should be replaced from time to time. (So, in some cases, should husbands!)

Cooking Fresh Vegetables

As there are in other aspects of cooking, so are there several schools of thought about the proper method of cooking vegetables. *I* believe in using very little water in most cases. In general, I also prefer to cook them quickly in plain water rather than stock, coating them as soon as they are done with sweet butter or margarine, kosher salt, and freshly ground pepper. A vegetable prepared in this way provides purity of flavor that I find unsurpassable. I serve combination vegetable dishes only with roasts or as a separate course.

Since I don't mind last-minute preparation, especially when cooking ahead may mean a loss of flavor, I often begin to cook a vegetable just before I call my guests to the table. If it is a variety that can be done very rapidly, I'll delay even longer. Believe me, it is worth training yourself to do this hasty kind of preparation.

Another heresy to which I occasionally subscribe is the addition of a pinch of bicarbonate of soda to peas, beans, broccoli, brussels sprouts, and cabbage. Nutritionists deplore the practice on the ground that it all but destroys the food value of these vegetables. I don't care. The soda keeps the vegetables green and flavorful. My eye and my palate comfort me in the presence of mine enemies!

Most vegetables should be cooked in a covered pan, with an inch or so of water. If you prefer *not* to add soda, cook them without a lid at least for the first minutes of the prescribed time, then put on a lid. However, remember that this procedure requires the use of a somewhat larger amount of water.

The smaller the vegetable, or the smaller the pieces of vegetable, the less water is needed. If you don't use soda, you should lift the lid three or four times to allow the vegetable gases to escape; unless you do this, they'll turn brown and look dreadful. (I find this a bore, which is why I use the soda.)

Whole vegetables need more time and more water, but don't drown them.

Except when you are cooking dried vegetables, you should add salt to the water. Some cooks like to add a pinch of sugar when they are preparing tomatoes, peas, or corn.

All vegetables ought to be cooked until they are just done; that is, cooked through but still retaining some of their original body.

Cooking Frozen Vegetables

I prepare frozen vegetables in a heavy enameled or copper pan with a lid. I use *at most* a couple of tablespoons of water, to which I normally add salt, butter, and soda, and cook (covered) at low heat, breaking up the frozen block with a fork and watching carefully to see that the portion of the frozen piece on the bottom isn't allowed to burn. At the end of the process, the water in the pan has usually evaporated. The use of so little water helps to preserve the illusion of "freshness."

Cooking Dried Vegetables

I should like to interpose here a few kind words about all manner of beans and lentils—both as main dishes and as side dishes. They abound in proteins, they're delicious, and they're cheap. It's a combination difficult to beat.

They ought to be rinsed thoroughly in cold water, then allowed to soak for 5 or 6 hours in a pan of cool water. After they have been drained, put them into boiling water, cook them for 2 minutes, allow them to rest in the hot water for an hour, and then bring them to a boil again and cook them slowly until they are done. Some are packaged so they do not need the long soak.

Steaming Vegetables

No method of preparing vegetables is better than steaming. It is more time consuming, but the quality is far superior to the usual hot-water technique. For the equipment required, see p. 63. A steamer is the best utensil, but there are substitutes.

I have not tried to compose a comprehensive list of vegetables and the methods for preparing them. My concern has been to illuminate some areas that occasion difficulties. Nor have I pointed out, until now, that many vegetables are at least as delicious when served cold as hot—as salads, for example, with *sauce vinaigrette* or mayonnaise. Finally, I've not treated here the preparation of vegetables by sautéing or braising, since these processes have already been covered in other sections.

Some Special Vegetables
ARTICHOKES

Artichokes may be served in three ways, as: an entire globe, of which you eat the tips of each exterior leaf; the whole tender leaves concealed within; and (after the removal of the "choke") the base or *fond*. You can buy the small, delicate center leaves in frozen or pickled form as artichoke "hearts." You can also purchase the *fonds* in tins, imported from France, at enormous cost. If you wish, however, you can also prepare *fonds* yourself in this manner:

Preparing Whole Artichokes: Cooks of various European countries use artichokes in many different ways, especially the very small ones. However, it is with the large types (though never too large) that I'm concerned here.

Slice off the stem in such a way that you also remove the bottom row of leaves, for these are very bitter. With a pair of scissors or a sharp knife cut off the tips of the remaining leaves so that the top is flattened. Artichokes should be cooked in water diluted with a lot of vinegar or lemon juice.

Don't try to keep them green.

The pan you use should be one that allows the artichokes to fit snugly, stems *up*. The reason for the snugness is to prevent them from bobbing around in the boiling water—thus possibly righting themselves and not cooking through. An alternative which is not ideal but one that works in a pinch: Place a heavy plate on top of the artichokes.

They should be about three-quarters immersed in the water and vinegar and cooked until the flesh of the bottom row of leaves (one of which you must pull off) is tender.

Artichokes may be served hot or cold, but always with a sauce. This may be hollandaise (especially when presented hot) or a lemon juice and butter sauce, good either for hot or cold artichokes. They are delicious when stuffed.

As well as eating the tender tips of the artichoke leaf, there are two additional portions that may be eaten with the leaves or used separately. The first is the heart, the tiny, tenderest leaves that sit just above the forbidding "choke." These may be consumed whole, unlike the outer leaves. You may buy them frozen and simply boil them and serve them with a *sauce vinaigrette*. They also are preserved this way in cans or jars.

Preparing Artichoke Hearts: Beneath the "choke" is the bottom or *fond*, which many think the pearl of this vegetable. It is almost as unctuous in flavor and texture as the avocado. To prepare your own, pare off the leaves and the "choke," the quilled material that tops the heart, and simmer the treasures in water, adding 2 tablespoons or so of flour, depending on the number of hearts you are preparing. If you save the exterior petals, you can fill them with peas or some other salad. The hearts are a wonderful garnish for a dish that is otherwise rather austere.

If your artichokes have browned with age, you may peel off the leaves in order to salvage the *fonds*. By keeping them covered with lemon juice as you prepare them, they will retain their flavor. Simmer them until tender, just covered with water to which you add 2 tablespoons or so of flour (the amount depending on the number of *fonds* being prepared), the lemon juice previously used, and salt and pepper. Keep them covered with liquid in your refrigerator until ready for use. *Fonds* may be purchased in cans for a price that will make your head reel!

ASPARAGUS

Asparagus must be washed in *warm* water, because the sandy soil in which it grows tends to lodge itself in the blossoms.

Never purchase asparagus that's wrinkled or whose blossom has begun to bloom.

A tiresome but extremely important first step in the preparation of asparagus is the careful peeling of the stalks. This offers the dual advantage of providing more of the stalk that is edible and removing the pockets of sand trapped in the immature leaves on the stem.

I tie asparagus in a bunch and place it standing upright in the bottom of a double boiler, using the top portion of the utensil reversed as a cover. In this fashion, the blossom ends are steamed and thoroughly cooked (without becoming mushy), while the stalks that stand in the boiling water are subjected to greater heat and can be eaten to a lower point than if the vegetable were cooked on its side. Though my asparagus sometimes turns slightly brown, I don't use soda in its preparation.

GREEN BEANS

The way you cut green beans will have a direct effect on their flavor. I don't know why this is so, and neither does anyone else. It *may* have to do with the manner in which the heated water is conveyed to the vegetable's fiber.

There are three basic ways of serving them: whole, diagonally or cross cut, or Frenched—sliced lengthwise (after removing the tips). Each provides a different flavor. If you are using beans in a sauce, the nature of the sauce will determine the way in which you prepare the beans. For example, beans *amandine* should be Frenched.

BEETS

Always leave about 2 inches of the stems on your beets. Boil them *in their skins*. Otherwise, they'll bleed to death. If you add vinegar to the water, it will brighten their beautiful color.

When beets are tender, run cold water over them (after they are cooked) until they are cool enough for you to handle them. Then you can simply slip the skins off. Cut them and dress them—that is, cover them with butter or sauce—and serve.

A better way than boiling large beets is to bake them. Be sure, however, not to pierce the skins, or they'll bleed. They should be baked in a medium oven for about 90 minutes, until they're tender. They'll look appalling when you remove them from the oven, but don't be upset. Peel them and cut them as you please. Served hot or cold, baked beets will delight and surprise you by how much better they taste than the boiled variety—despite their ghastly shrunken appearance as they come out of the oven.

To many, beet tops are a delicacy. They should be prepared in the way you cook spinach.

BROCCOLI

The purchase of frozen broccoli strikes me as no end of a waste of money. As with asparagus, never buy fresh broccoli whose buds have started to flower.

Like asparagus, too, the peeling of the stems will afford you more edible material.

Broccoli may be cooked whole. If you choose this method, slash the main stems to speed their cooking time. You may also break broccoli up into flowerets, slicing off the stems and cutting them up into diagonal pieces. Give these a head start of 2 or 3 minutes before placing the flowerets in the boiling water, for they take longer to cook.

I prepare broccoli in a medium amount of salted water—i.e., filling the pan so that the water covers about half of the vegetable.

CABBAGE

In the earlier portion of this chapter, I made some observations about what to look for in a good head of cabbage. Your home needn't smell like an old boardinghouse when it is being prepared—provided that you just simmer the vegetable instead of bringing it to a rolling boil. Use as little water as possible. I add pinches of soda and salt to the water.

CARROTS

As with green beans, the way you choose to cut (or *not* to cut) carrots will help to determine their final cooked flavor. Add a pinch of sugar to the salted water in which you cook them.

It is important that the carrots be neither too large nor too old.

Grated raw carrots make a delicious salad, dressed with *sauce vinaigrette*.

CELERY

It is preferable to scrape the fibers from celery with a sharp paring knife rather than with a peeler.

Braised celery is an excellent cooked vegetable, especially delicious when served with fowl.

CELERY ROOT OR CELERIAC

A root of the celery family, usually served cold or in soups.

SWEET CORN

You shouldn't add salt to the water in which sweet corn is cooked. Instead, put in a touch of sugar. Copious quantities of water should be used, and it should be at a full rolling boil before you immerse the ears of corn in it. Cooking time is about 7 minutes—not a second more than 8.

I've already had my say about the need for sweet corn to be as fresh as possible—direct from patch to pot.

When you are serving corn, don't allow it to wait at the table for you; better to wait at the table for the corn. Try using it alone as a first course. Not only does this make it easier to serve at the moment of perfection, but it offers this vegetable the solo position it deserves when it is truly fresh. It should be eaten with salt, pepper, and butter (preferably sweet butter).

CUCUMBERS

There are at least two ways of preparing cucumbers. One is to soak them for 30 minutes in ice water, then dress them. The French method is to place them in a colander, sprinkle them carefully with salt, and weigh them down with a plate so that the liquid which forms as the result of the addition of the salt may drain off. Do this for an hour. Rinse them in cold water and dry them off before dressing them.

My own preference is for the French way, because it eliminates the slightly unpleasant bitter flavor—and though I can't prove it, I suspect this method makes the cucumbers somewhat more digestible.

Cooked cucumbers can offer an interesting variation in the prepared vegetable line. They merit investigation.

Never buy a cucumber that's limp.

EGGPLANTS

Unless I'm going to use them in a casserole dish (which I usually do), I salt and press eggplants in the same way I prepare cucumbers.

Avoid purchasing an eggplant that seems to you unusually light. This means it has been allowed to dry out.

ENDIVE

Rinse it in cool water, wipe it dry, and pull off the leaves, one by one. With *sauce vinaigrette* it makes one of the great salads. If you like a bitter-tasting vegetable, braised endive is for you.

FENNEL

Though it is an herb, the fennel bulb may be served as a vegetable—boiled, braised, or raw in salads.

KOHLRABI

This is a member of the cabbage family, a curious-looking, bulbous vegetable. The main stem forms a ball from which strands emerge in great disorder. The bulb is what you eat —boiled, and consumed when young and fresh.

JERUSALEM ARTICHOKES

They are not artichokes at all, but tubers. Peeling them presents some difficulties, but they have their rewards as a flavoring for soups or even as a separate vegetable dish. And they make wonderful pickles!

LEEKS

Leeks should be split lengthwise and washed under running water in order to clean them thoroughly. They are a necessity for certain soups, and may be served as a separate vegetable as well.

MUSHROOMS

It is often worth the trouble to remove the stems of mushrooms and to peel them, for the stems and peelings are useful for making stuffings and essences. Simmered for a couple of hours, pressed through a sieve to extract as much of their flavor as possible, the stems and peelings make an excellent broth which can also be used to add mushroom taste to stocks and sauces.

ONIONS

The onion family is remarkably extensive, and heaven only knows what cooking would be like without it—whether as flavoring for the dry martini or as the principal ingredient in soup or onion sandwich, the latter a delight of middle Europe and Russia. For eating as a boiled vegetable, the small white onion is best. The larger Bermuda variety is preferable for serving raw, as is the beautiful purple Spanish type which I like best for onion soup, though the yellow onion is satisfactory for this purpose too.

If you suffer when peeling onions, try doing it in cold water; this reduces the intensity of the fumes. If you want the juice of an onion, cut one in half and press it in a squeezer, as you would a lemon or orange.

POTATOES

Potatoes should be boiled in their jackets—if you are going to boil them at all. If you *must* peel potatoes before boiling them, be sure to boil them until just done. Otherwise, they decompose.

New potatoes are preferable for plain boiling or steaming. Old potatoes, however, are good for boiling if you plan to use them cold—as for potato salad.

The Idaho potato is the best for baking. I place skewers through potatoes before baking them. This helps to transmit the heat evenly and causes them to cook more rapidly. I dislike the flabby skin that results from baking a potato in foil.

TOMATOES

If you want to ripen tomatoes, *don't* place them in the sun. Keep them in a closed brown paper bag until suitable for serving.

To peel a tomato, drop it into boiling water for about a

minute. This will cause the skin to come away easily from the meat.

As with some other vegetables, the manner of slicing makes a difference to a tomato's flavor. In the same way, peeled tomatoes taste different from unpeeled ones. I don't know why.

One of the most satisfying ways of preparing tomatoes (other than the beefsteak variety) is to slice them vertically, unpeeled, very thinly and dress them with a *sauce vinaigrette*. If you don't have a tomato knife, use a blade that is sharp but knicked in a few places to facilitate the breaking of the skin.

Some recipes call for seeded tomatoes. To remove the seeds, slice the tomato in half horizontally and perform the operation with a fork or a small spoon.

STARCHES: GRAINS, PASTA, RICE, BEANS, PEAS, LENTILS, AND CHICKPEAS

With all of these products, it is usually wise to follow the advice offered on the packages they come in. The important point to remember is that it is almost impossible to cook any of these products without causing them to stick if you fail to use large amounts of water and salt.

The main trick for the successful cooking of pasta, rice, and dried beans is to use at least 4 cups of water for each ½ cup of the dried product. Add salt to the water at the beginning with pasta and rice. In the case of pasta, a few tablespoons of oil are helpful to prevent sticking.

Salt should be added only at the end of the cooking process of dried beans and peas, because salt tends to toughen their outer skins.

Cooking Rice

An alternative method of cooking rice is *rissole*—made with little water. Follow the recipe in a cookbook you have confidence in. The flavor is different from that of the fluffy rice produced with lots of water.

It will hardly surprise you to learn of my hostility to precooked rice. It may, as the advertisements assure you, never produce a failure—but it will never produce a triumph, either. I prefer long-grained rice, rinsed in cold water (in a sieve). Allow water to pour over it until it runs completely clear. Then cook it in a large pot with plenty of water, amply salted. Stir it frequently with a fork. When the rice is *just done* (a little nubbly to the teeth—not pasty), drain it and place it in a colander that fits in the pot in which it was cooked. Put it back on the stove with a little water in the pot and allow it to steam gently until you are ready to serve it. Since the pot I use for rice is a handsome one, I bring it to the table, colander and all.

Pilaf of rice calls for all the moisture to be absorbed by the grains. The liquid can be water or stock. I use one of several good recipes. There are many.

For variety, it is sometimes pleasant to substitute rice or kasha (whole wheat grains) for pasta or potatoes.

Don't forget that leftover rice and macaroni make excellent salads. They may also be used to make good leftover dishes by the addition of a fresh sauce. As a matter of fact, it is not a bad policy always to cook a lot more of these products than you need for a single meal, just to have them for other dishes. This is a handy way of saving both time and fuel.

FRUITS

The proper approach to the selection of acceptable fruit is identical to that of good vegetables. Occasionally, some supermarkets have nice fruit, but it is usually more reliable and certainly more satisfactory to locate a grocer who knows fruit and specializes in it. His prices will be higher, but what you think you save when you buy mainly on the basis of price is lost in waste—not to mention flavor.

The difficulty I've found in exurban Connecticut and Upstate New York is in obtaining properly ripened fruit. Attempting to ripen fruit on your own is a very chancy business, but sometimes leaving it in a brown paper bag, as with tomatoes, works. You must adapt your menu arrangements to the availability of fruit—electing at the last minute to serve pineapple for dessert instead of custard. If only two or three days of ripening are necessary, this may be a safe undertaking, especially if you have a place in which to do it well. If not, the likelihood is that you'll succeed in spoiling more fruit than you ripen.

As I have indicated repeatedly, I would rather pay the additional price and not have to be anxious. This is particularly true of melons. I am willing (even eager) to pay a high price for a perfect melon or to do without melon altogether in preference to being stuck with one that is bland and tasteless.

Another advantage of frequenting a shop that specializes in fine fruit is that you need have no hesitancy about complaining when you've not received what you paid for. No matter what the management of the supermarkets says, you'll not get much satisfaction if you register a complaint about the quality of produce. It is all hopeless and dehumanized. Everyone in a supermarket is in league with that big computer in the sky.

When no decent fresh fruits are available, you do have a choice of preserved varieties. The canned ones have, of course, a quite different flavor from the fresh and, so far as I'm concerned, they are a very poor substitute. Some cooks don't mind this; I mind it very much. But by perusing cookbooks such as the one by Elizabeth David, you will find some good dessert recipes that call for canned fruits.

In winter, I prefer to use dried fruit—or apples and pears in season. I find a great pleasure in making dried fruit desserts: stewed prunes and/or apricots, for instance, cooked in wine, sometimes served with rice, sometimes in tarts, or simply with whipped cream. They are economical, tasty, and worth investigating.

However, my fundamental outlook about fruits is the same as about vegetables. They are best eaten fresh in their respective seasons.

13

Parsing: *How to Read a Recipe*

You Have to Think in the Kitchen

Question: Do you *think* while you're cooking? Despite your reflex to respond immediately in the affirmative, try to consider.

Let me explain why I pose the question. It has been my experience, after sitting around the kitchens of friends for many years, that they have somehow contrived to train themselves *not* to think about what they are doing in the kitchen—that most of what they do, indeed, in any part of the house, is a form of sleepwalking.

I am not certain why this should be so. Perhaps it is because many people, especially women, have the impression that the jobs to be done around the house require no thought and are really not worthwhile. In the case of cooking, it may be that they don't *understand* what they are doing, and are thus tied to the apron strings of master chefs. I hope, as this book nears its conclusion, that this is no longer true for *you*.

Whatever the explanation, if you can honestly count yourself in the number of the thoughtless cooks, wise up—and wake up! You'll never enjoy cooking or any other form of housework as much as you deserve if you refuse to apply your intelligence to it. The use of intelligence precludes boredom.

The men and women renowned for their talents in the kitchen are mainly those who have made cooking their hobby. All of us tend to take our hobbies very seriously. That is why I invariably refer to myself as a "serious" and not a "gourmet" cook—the latter expression having more *éclat*, perhaps, but less meaning.

Since most of us *have* to spend many hours of our lives cooking, why *not* take it seriously and, by applying our minds to the process, derive greater pleasure from it. As an avocation, cooking has a lot to recommend it: beauty, taste, rhythmic motions, and excited anticipation. Besides, it is a pleasure which can be created alone, or in the company of others. And there are few hobbies that can afford so much joy to those about us.

Observe! Think! You'll be far richer for the experience.

Approaching a Recipe

During the past year I've been conducting an informal poll of friends, asking those who enjoy cooking and those who don't just how they approach a particular recipe. Most of them admitted that they had never really thought about it. And this omission discloses the initial difficulty. Just as you should think about your cooking, so should you think beforehand about the recipes you intend to follow. If you don't consult them thoroughly before you begin to prepare them, you may easily find yourself in a dreadful tangle.

It may seem obvious that you should read through every recipe you plan to use for a given meal before you go shopping. It *is* obvious. But I'm astonished at the frequency of cooks' discovering, after returning from market, that a critical ingredient is missing. Another reason for reading your recipes in advance is that you'll know just how much time you have to allow for preparation.

In cookbooks, the presentation of recipes varies a great deal from one to another. Some admirable volumes place unnecessary obstacles in the reader's path by burying the required ingredients in the body of what amounts to a descriptive essay about the dish. Others, wonderfully organized, are so full of helpful hints that they obscure (and occasionally omit mention of) the basic needs. Of all the general cookbooks I'm familiar with, *The New York Times Cookbook*, by Craig Claiborne, is outstanding for its clarity and organization. The ingredients are presented in the order of their use, and the body of the recipe is laid out simply, step by step. It is so easy to use that I think it ought to be the key volume in any kitchen library. (For other cookbooks that have pleased me over the years I've devoted to this subject, I refer you to the Opinionated Bibliography, p. 213.)

The two volumes of *Mastering the Art of French Cooking* have a unique recipe plan which some readers find helpful and others are confused by. I suspect the format is more trying for old cooking hands than for novices, for the experienced cook isn't accustomed to so great a detailing of the steps as is offered by these otherwise admirable books.

READING A RECIPE

As I observed at the very beginning of this book, almost all recipes are composed in a form of grammatical shorthand. What I hope you have derived from reading it is a greater fluency, a mastery of the grammar of the kitchen.

Now to the crunch: how to read a recipe.

Take the time to familiarize yourself with the one you have chosen. It is impossible to cook in a rhythmical, relaxed manner if you must constantly refer back to the cookbook.

A Demonstration Recipe

The recipe I've selected to demonstrate the points I've been making in this book is for a dish I like very much and serve frequently—a stuffed shoulder of lamb. As it happens, this offers examples of several difficulties cooks commonly encounter. The author, Louis Diat, was one of the greatest French chefs ever to establish himself permanently in the United States, head chef of the Ritz in New York, and principal compiler of the early cookbooks published by *Gourmet*. This recipe, however, is taken from his own book, *French Cooking for Americans*. The dish described is a delicious sample of "plain" French cooking:

Stuffed Shoulder of Lamb

    1 lamb shoulder, boned
    2–3 tablespoons of good fat
    1 onion, chopped fine
    ½ pound sausage meat, or leftover cooked meat, chopped fine
    1 tablespoon chopped parsley
    1 tablespoon flour
    1 egg
    1 cup fresh bread crumbs
    ½ teaspoon salt
    A little pepper
    1 onion, sliced
    1 carrot, sliced
    1 faggot [parsley, thyme, and bay leaf, tied together]

Mix together sausage, cooked onion, parsley, bread crumbs, egg, salt and pepper and stuff the shoulder with this mixture. Roll up the shoulder and tie it with string. Spread the sliced onion and carrot in the bottom of a roasting pan and add the faggot. Rub stuffed shoulder with a little salt and pepper, spread with good fat and put on top of vegetables in roasting pan. Bake, uncovered, in a moderately hot oven of 425° about 30 minutes, turning it often to brown it on all sides. Sprinkle flour on top of the vegetables, add 1 cup hot water, cover pan, and continue cooking at moderate heat of 375° to

400° about 2 hours. If water cooks away, add more. Discard faggot. Remove meat and vegetables to serving dish. Strain gravy and skim off fat. Serves 6.

After the first reading of this recipe you'll find that you must make three decisions before you do your shopping:

1. If you are unable to purchase a boned shoulder of lamb, will you have the time and the knowledge to bone one yourself? We will assume that you plan to do the boning.
2. If you have leftover meat, do you prefer to use it or to buy sausage for the purpose? I prefer to use sausage, reserving leftover meats for other dishes.
3. Are you going to grind fresh bread crumbs, as Diat suggests, or will you buy them? We'll take it that you have some stale bread on hand, so you're planning to make your own crumbs.

Since there is quite a bit of advance preparation involved in this dish, I usually serve it on Sunday for an evening dinner. This gives me the whole day for leisurely attention to boning the shoulder, grinding the bread crumbs, and reading *The New York Times*. After I've finished the boning, I sit down with a cup of coffee and a cigarette as I reread the recipe, thinking about it as I do. The following is a rough approximation of the thoughts that go through my mind at this time:

Let's see. The cooking time is 30 minutes for browning and 2 hours for the rest of the cooking process. Which process is involved, roasting or braising? Braising. That means it should occupy the middle shelf of the oven. Two and a half hours of total cooking time, plus another 30 minutes for the remainder of the preparation. If dinner is to be at 7, I should be in the kitchen at 4. Better allow 15 minutes or so longer, just to be on the safe side. So I'll start cooking at 3:45. If I find I'm ahead of schedule, I can delay putting the shoulder into the oven.

What to do first? The bread crumbs. Since I'm not rushed, I'll use a round stone to do the crushing instead of the blender. The bread is dry enough so I don't have to put it in the oven first.

I'm going to use sausage. Diat doesn't say anything about precooking it, but he does mention cooking the onion. If I fail to precook the sausage, its fat and the fat of the lamb will mean that there will be lots of fat in the roasting pan. So I'll sauté the sausage first, using a fork to crumble it. Then, when it's almost done, I'll drain off the excess fat and add the onion to cook.

Then what? I'll need to cool that combination a bit before adding the bread crumbs, egg, parsley, salt, and pepper, or the egg will cook. I'll just mix them in the sautéing pan. After that I'll stuff and tie the shoulder. Better be certain I have string handy in the kitchen. I'll check on that right now.

What's next? Ah, a mirepoix. Diat doesn't tell me to sauté it, but I shall. For the "good fat" I'll use what I've saved in the referigator from the last stock I made.

Diat says I should brown the meat in the oven, but I think I'll brown it in the roasting pan on top of the stove, before I cook the mirepoix, instead of following his advice. Then I'll remove the meat, sauté the mirepoix, and mix the flour and hot water with the mirepoix before putting the meat back in the pan. Since it's a braising recipe, I'll baste the shoulder and then put the lid on.

That means I should set the oven at 375° and increase the cooking time by about 15 minutes, since I won't have browned it in the oven at the beginning. I'll only turn the shoulder over once during the cooking.

That's more or less the sort of soliloquy I *consciously* rehearse before I start to prepare a dish. It's neither Lady Macbeth's nor Molly Bloom's, but believe me, it serves a very useful purpose.

Dealing with the Unexpected

No matter how tested and true a recipe, you may discover yourself short of butter, short of liquid, and wondering what you should do to remedy such a problem. Again, these are instances when you shouldn't panic, but use your head. Just make the additions you think necessary, but do it gradually and cautiously. Make a note in your cookbook so you are forewarned the next time.

I was making a moussaka not long ago. It demanded twice as much butter as the recipe called for. The reason was that I was using a larger pan than the one the author of the recipe had in mind.

The point here is not to allow yourself to become a slave to the letter of the recipe. Think, and keep your cool. Most professionals work only rarely from written recipes; mainly, they cook from experience, as pilots used to fly by the seats of their pants. This is what you must learn to do—to develop your instincts and intuitions, both products of experience.

When you encounter a problem, think it through. If something burns, don't worry about it. Try to figure out what you did wrong. Throw the dish away and serve your guests a good omelet, or open a can of corned beef hash. Every cook has failures. Just the other day, I burned some pork chops in a brand-new Dutch oven. It was my own fault. Not being familiar with the characteristics of the utensil, I should have been paying closer attention to what was happening. I'll know better next time.

Use common sense. If something looks too dry to you, add some liquid. If it seems excessively fatty, pour off the superfluous fat. Consider recipes as guides, not as sources of divine revelation. You'll enjoy cooking much more that way.

A sense of humor, combined with a sense of self-preservation, will be helpful in emergencies. Always have something tucked away on your shelf in the event of crisis. You'll hope you'll never need it—like hurricane lamps or candles in case of a power failure—but it's nice to have that feeling of security. False pride has no place in the kitchen—or anywhere else.

My husband, early in our marriage, devised a formula for explaining failure and success to dinner guests when I served something I'd prepared for the first time. If it didn't come out right, I was to say, "I don't understand it. I've been cooking that for years and this is the first time it's done that." If, on the other hand, it was splendid, *he* was to say, "You know, that's the first time Carol ever cooked this."

14

Rhyming:
*Menu Planning
and
Serving Suggestions*

A Formal Setting

For most of us today, the sort of formal dinner party that my parents used to give is a rarity: a long table which seated eighteen guests in matching chairs, a real lace tablecloth, with antique Bristol glass and Dresden china table decorations, bowls overflowing with lovely fresh fruit or flowers. Between courses one was never left without a service plate. Three maids used to provide an almost magical service of these dinners; my father thought a butler pretentious. In the late twenties, after breaking the bank at Monte Carlo, my father trifled with the idea of purchasing Mother an amethyst and diamond necklace and finally abandoned the idea because, he explained, they would then have to employ a butler and thus be compelled to renounce the "simplicity" of their present social life! As a matter of fact, we did have one male servant, who did the heavy cleaning once a week and who came in on the evenings of large dinner parties to wash the dishes as the meal progressed. It was before the era of the reliable dishwashing machine, and there wasn't enough china to get us through a five-course meal for eighteen.

One of my roles as a child in these great events was to help Mother plan the menus. June Platt's *Party Cook Book* would be brought down from her bedroom. Later, I assisted the cook in preparing the main course. My parents were rightly renowned for their delightful dinner parties and, especially, for the delicious food they served and for what the French call its *présentation*.

My First Dinner Party

By the time I was eighteen, I felt myself an expert in these matters, as a result of my apprenticeship in my mother's house. I had prepared and served my own dinner parties. My idea then of a perfect meal was a first course of smoked salmon, followed by green turtle and pea soup, *poulet patron* (a rich chicken dish made with cream, mushrooms, and truffles—still a favorite), rice, string beans, a salad, and a dessert of *crêpes Suzette*. All of the recipes came from that first book of June Platt's. I was enormously proud and very sure of myself.

It was at about this time that two events occurred that were to affect my future life. I read M. F. K. Fisher's *The Gastronomical Me*. In that book I learned that one's entire attitude toward food could become a significant aspect of daily life, not simply reserved for special occasions. My natural interest and preoccupation with cooking were thus broadened and began to assume the dimensions they now represent for me.

The second significant event was my encounters with Alan and Kenneth Hall, who were very successful London restaurateurs. Wine and food were their business and also their favorite diversion. They flattered me in the most seductive ways. They took *my* interest in these things as seriously as they did their own. I became their eager and devoted student. It would be impossible for me to exaggerate their importance in my schooling. They introduced me to the systematic study of wines—which opened an entirely new door of the house of gastronomical pleasure. Though there is undoubtedly a good deal to be learned about wine from books, it is ultimately only by tasting that one gains the necessary experience—and the accompanying delight.

Of course, much talk went along with the food and drink, and all of it seemed wonderful to me. One day, I boasted to Kenneth about my perfect meal—the one noted above. In the kindliest way, he led me one step farther along the road to an understanding of food. No matter how fine each of those dishes might be, he told me, the menu I'd put together was unsatisfactory. I was crushed and mystified. How could that be, if every item was perfectly prepared?

MENU PLANNING

This was Kenneth Hall's point: Regardless of how good each dish is, a meal—that is, a *menu*—must be considered as an entity, an entirety. A well-planned dinner is analogous to painting a picture. Each element must have a direct relationship with all the other elements in the composition. Kenneth was right; I'd bungled miserably.

Why? Well, first I served a salmon. Then there was turtle in my soup. The two flavors were too closely akin to each other, both being from the sea. There were peas in the soup, and I had followed them with green beans. Would I, he inquired gently, serve peas and beans together in the same course (except, perhaps, cold in a salad)? Of course not. Yet presenting them in sequence amounted to the same thing.

From this initial lesson in menu planning, Kenneth led me carefully through some others. When we dined in restaurants, he would order the meal and, as he did, he explained his reasons for making particular selections.

Menumaking occasionally stumps everyone. This is a reason why menu cookbooks are so popular, though I confess that after considering some of the meals suggested, I'm revolted by the combinations proposed and the order in which they are laid out. Nevertheless, though I think myself exceptionally competent in most aspects of cooking (pastry and breads aside), I still trouble a lot about the menu of every meal I prepare.

The time and thought I devote to this aspect of cooking is way out of proportion to the time I give to the actual preparation of the food. I keep a detailed record of every dinner party we give. Not only do I write down who was present, but also where each guest sat at the table, and—of course—what I served. In this way, when a guest returns for another party I try not to duplicate any portion of the meal he or she has been served before. It is not merely a matter of pride (though I confess that is part of it), I like the idea of surprising friends with dishes I've not offered them previously. The one exception is when I serve a favorite dish to a favorite guest.

To a degree, I'm influenced as well by the experience of dining out. We will go to the house of friends and, nine times out of ten, be served the same dishes time after time —simply because the hostess hasn't taken the trouble to keep a record of what she prepared for us on previous visits. I don't know why, but in one house the dish is usually lamb, which I like, but when it's presented repeatedly, it becomes a bore. Variety is essential.

Choosing Your Courses

I've said it before and I'll say it again: The common procedure is to begin with the dish you plan to be the focal point of the meal. As a rule, this will be the principal dish, though there are occasions when this may not be so, as when you know, for instance, that one of your guests is crazy about a special soup or dessert. In that event, all other elements of the meal must be made to harmonize with *that*.

Assuming that the main course *is* the essential factor, build backward and forward from it, keeping in mind that it is desirable to offer contrasting flavors, colors, ingredients, and textures. Even the mixture of hot and cold dishes should be taken into account. Repetitions are to be avoided, as is an excess of starches.

The hardest kind of dish to plan around is one that involves a cream sauce. It means that you can't serve a cream soup or practically any other liquid except, perhaps, a clear soup. You can't serve a cold fish or a *pâté*, or *oeufs en gelée*, or shrimps, or oysters. Nor can you follow a cream-sauce dish with a dessert that in any way resembles the *first* course—a very limiting condition, but one that the imaginative cook can cope with by offering a fruit or a cake that is not too rich, thus providing the needed contrast.

Once you have chosen the main course, remember that the items to accompany it must be in balance and harmony with it. If it is elaborate, a simply cooked vegetable is a good partner. If it is a roast or a steak, fancily prepared vegetables would be appropriate. If you serve an elaborate vegetable dish with the main course, don't offer a first course of vegetable soup. Choice of starches should be made on the same basis.

If you are serving a fine wine, a cheese course is a particularly nice selection. However, don't serve cheese as a separate course if cheese is used in another dish. A sprinkling of cheese is permissible, but not a cheese dish or a strong cheese sauce.

For dessert, the choice depends—as does everything else in the well-planned meal—on what else you've served. If the menu has been heavy (or seems so to you), cooked or raw fruit is a good option. If you want to serve a rich dessert, keep the other portions of the meal simple and austere. It is wise to recall, at all events, that the dessert rings down the curtain on your dinner drama. It is the last speech you make. It should assuage your guests' desire for something sweet, and, at the same time, be in tune with what you have already served them. You want them rising from the table in a state of supreme sensual well-being—not feeling stuffed, bloated, torpid, and miserable.

A well-planned meal, served in pleasant surroundings and with ease, is in its fashion a gratifying experience to be shared with friends.

Some of My Favorite Menus

I remarked earlier that I keep records of every dinner party I've given. Here are some special menus drawn from that notebook:

A seated wedding breakfast for sixteen:
  Brunswick stew (June Platt's recipe), made with chicken and heavy cream—unctuous, a great American dish
  Orange ice (homemade)
  A three-tiered pound cake (June Platt). The top layer was baked in a ring pan. Daisies, poppies, and bachelors' buttons were placed in the hole.

A dinner for a friend of my father's who had just become a *Chevalier du Tastevin:*
  Fresh tomato soup (Elizabeth David)
  Pâté en croûte (Louis Diat), served with a white Hermitage wine
  Duck with turnips (June Platt), accompanied by a green salad with Dijon mustard dressing, and a red Château Pape Clément wine
  Peach soufflé (Craig Claiborne) served with a Jurançon

doux wine, slightly less sweet (and *much* less expensive) than Château d' Yquem

A family dinner:
Cauliflower soup (Elizabeth David)
Meat loaf (my own), served with green beans and mashed potatoes
Chocolate mousse (Samuel Chamberlain)

Good friends, #1:
Shrimp soup (Germaine Carter)
Boiled leg of lamb with sauce béarnaise (June Platt), with gnocchi (June Platt) and cold asparagus *polonaise* (my own)
Strawberries with cream cheese sauce (my own)

Good friends, #2:
Celery soup (my own)
Roast chicken tarragon (classic French), with home-fried potato chips
Bibb lettuce with a dressing of the juice from the chicken (Elizabeth David's suggestion)
Pears Carol (my own)

SERVING SUGGESTIONS

Once my menu is established, the real work involved in the preparation of a dinner party is over for me. But how I labor over those menus!

The first consideration should be the amount of time you have in which to prepare the meal, the season of the year, and the availability of the meat and produce you'd like to serve. The best meal in the world can be wrecked if the hosts are tense or absent for a good part of the time getting things ready for their guests. After all, entertaining friends and feeding one's own family should be periods of communion between people.

Admonitions

If you are having a large number of guests, don't serve too many courses, and don't prepare something that is difficult to make. With cocktails, serve hors d'oeuvres for munching—biscuits and cheese, potato chips, olives, or salted nuts. (Note: Do *not* serve cheese before a meal if you are offering a cheese course for dinner.) Raw vegetables make a good appetizer, but I add the identical caveat: Don't duplicate and thus overshadow the dinner vegetable by serving it initially as an appetizer or hors d'oeuvre. A smoked or pickled fish is also satisfactory for this purpose, again provided you are not serving fish for dinner.

Don't offer too much of anything to eat with the preprandial drinks. You can easily spoil the appetites of your guests for the meal you've toiled over. Moreover, if you devote too much attention to this peripheral aspect of the party, you'll perhaps not have given enough time and thought to the meal itself. After all, the two principal objectives of serving food with cocktails is to prevent your guests from starving to death before dinner is served and to keep them from getting drunk. You should want to build a bit of drama into your dinner, so it is wise to start the evening off quietly, building the excitement as you progress.

There may be occasions when it is convenient to serve the first course of a meal with cocktails in the living room. If so, make the fact perfectly clear to your guests. *Remember, the food served with cocktails or aperitifs should be considered in relation to the meal you plan and to the amount of time you have allowed for its preparation.*

Serving

Serving should be considered in the terms I've mentioned before: How can a meal be most gracefully and graciously presented? If you can afford a domestic and can find one who is not more trouble than help, well and good. There are, however, some other and cheaper aids to serving. An important one is a sideboard or a service table.

Don't compel your guests to select their seats. It always occasions confusion and embarrassment—emotions you want no one to feel in your home. If you don't want to use place cards, make a table chart and guide your guests to their allocated spots.

Have the first course on the table when your guests sit down. If you use a sideboard or buffet, ask them to deposit soiled dishes on it and to serve themselves the main course. Let dessert service be from your own hand. The idea is for the meal to pass smoothly, with as few interruptions (like bobbing up and down) as you can manage.

My personal method of serving is to make use of a rolling restaurant wagon with two shelves. I serve everything from this, gathering the soiled dishes and stacking them on the lower shelf as I pass each new course on to the guests from the top. I always have the initial course waiting for them when they reach the table. Only *I* am allowed to get up during the meal, though my husband serves the wine. I make only one trip to the kitchen, to get the dessert. In this way, I'm able to serve twelve guests seated at a table. Another advantage of this method is that all the dirty dishes are neatly stacked on my wagon, ready for washing, and not scattered over every available kitchen surface.

An Opinion About Buffet Dinners

The buffet dinner is a peeve of mine. In my opinion, unless you have tables at which your guests can sit and places designated for them, the buffet dinner is just one small cut higher in the classification of entertainment than the cocktail party. I think I've heard all the standard apologies for them—the chief one being that one owes so many people for so many meals that there is just no other way of paying them all back in a bunch. The buffet dinner is fatiguing to the guests, destructive of conversation (which is so important an element to the successful dinner party), and denigrating to the food you have lovingly prepared. The better the food, the more insulting is this kind of service to it. It is just as deadly to good food as allowing the cocktail period to run on too long.

Preparation Time

When you are planning your menu, take into account the time at your disposal. Above all, as I remarked before, stay relaxed. If you don't mind making a *béarnaise* or a hollandaise sauce, you can disappear from the table after the first course (or *during* it, if you eat rapidly or skip it altogether). No one will notice if you *alone* are absent for just a few minutes.

Give some thought to a course of cold fish or cold asparagus or some other cold dish, especially if time is a crucial factor at any point in the preparation of the meal. An oven-cooked vegetable is another easy dish for last-minute preparation and service. Green salads have become so common a course that it would be pleasant to find an adequate substitute—or even omit it entirely.

In the house we now occupy, I have a large kitchen with several comfortable chairs in it and a table at one end that seats eight, with a much larger table in an adjacent area for bigger gatherings. I love this, for it means I can cook anything I please, no matter how time-consuming and elaborate, for I'm not separated from the guests. I can get up occasionally to visit the stove without interrupting the flow of the conversation or of the meal.

The Way I Do It

Depending on the type of party I'm giving, I do one of two things to give myself adequate preparation time. We often serve cocktails in the kitchen, while I proceed with the cooking. This, of course, is for less formal occasions. For most parties, however, I allow time for the guests to have a couple of drinks in the living room. Halfway through their consumption of the first one, I go quietly to the kitchen area to complete the preparations. Because I love to have company when I'm working, I often ask one or two guests to come along with me—if the party is large enough to allow for that. They and I rejoin the general gathering when dinner is served. After the meal, my husband prepares and serves the coffee and digestive libations.

If you have neither spouse nor companion, select a friend who enjoys entertaining to act as your co-host or hostess in this role.

A Concluding Thought

James Stephens put an aphorism in the mouths of women in *The Crock of Gold:* "The art of packing is the last lecture of wisdom." Being an Irishman, poor Stephens never knew that it is *really* the art of cooking.

APPENDICES

APPENDIX I

Weights and Measures in the United States and Great Britain

Liquid Measures

UNITED STATES		GREAT BRITAIN
1¼ teaspoon	=	1 teaspoon
1½ tablespoon	=	1 tablespoon
1 tablespoon	=	1 dessert spoon
⅚ gill	=	1 gill
⅚ pint	=	1 pint
⅚ quart	=	1 quart
⅚ gallon	=	1 gallon

Temperature Measures

FAHRENHEIT		REGLO
240°–310° (low)	=	¼–2
320°–370° (moderate)	=	3–4
380°–400° (fairly hot)	=	5
410°–440° (hot)	=	6–7
450°–480° (very hot)	=	8–9

Appendix I

Odd Measures

1 claret glass	=	6 tablespoons
1 Bordeaux glass	=	1 deciliter
1 liqueur glass	=	½ ounce or 1 tablespoon

Bulk Measures

2 cups butter	=	1 pound
2 cups sugar	=	1 pound
4½ cups flour	=	1 pound
8 tablespoons	=	¼ pound butter or ½ cup
½ pint cream	=	1 cup

Mixtures with Egg

1 egg yolk will sustain ½ cup oil
1 egg yolk will sustain ¼ pound butter or margarine

Egg Measures (approximate)

1 cup of whole eggs	=	7 small eggs 6 medium eggs 5 large eggs 4 extra large eggs
1 cup of whites	=	10 small 8 medium 7 large 6 extra large
1 cup of yolks	=	18 small 16 medium 14 large 12 extra large
10 medium eggs	=	1 pound

American Weights and Measures

1 teaspoon	=	⅓ tablespoon
1 tablespoon	=	½ fluid ounce
2 tablespoons	=	⅛ cup
16 tablespoons	=	1 cup
1 cup	=	½ pint
2 pints	=	1 quart
4 quarts	=	1 gallon
8 quarts (bulk)	=	1 peck
4 pecks	=	1 bushel

CONVERSION OF UNITED STATES MEASURES TO THE METRIC SYSTEM

Dry Measures

OUNCES	GRAMS	GRAMS	OUNCES
1	28.35	1	.035
2	56.7	2	.07
3	85.05	3	.11
4	113.40	4	.14
5	141.75	5	.18
6	170.1	6	.21
7	198.45	7	.25
8	226.8	8	.28
9	255.15	9	.32
10	283.5	10	.35
11	311.85	11	.39
12	340.2	12	.42
13	368.55	13	.46
14	396.9	14	.49
15	425.25	15	.53
16 (1 lb.)	453.6	16	.57

POUNDS	KILOGRAMS	KILOGRAMS	POUNDS
1	.454	1	2.2
2	.91	2	4.4
3	1.36	3	6.6
4	1.81	4	8.8
5	2.27	5	11.00
6	2.72	6	13.2
7	3.18	7	15.4
8	3.63	8	17.6
9	4.08	9	19.8
10	4.54	10	22.00

Liquid Measures

OUNCES	MILLILITERS	MILLILITERS	OUNCES
1	29.6	1	.035
2	59.15	2	.07
3	88.7	3	.10
4	118.3	4	.14
5	147.9	5	.17
6	177.4	6	.20
7	207.00	7	.24
8	236.6	8	.27
9	266.2	9	.30
10	297.6	10	.33

QUARTS	LITERS	LITERS	QUARTS
1	.95	1	1.06
2	1.9	2	2.1
3	2.8	3	3.2
4	3.8	4	4.2

APPENDIX II

Kitchen Equipment

When I was eighteen, I moved to New York to attend design school and rented an apartment in the house of Nell and Albert Boni on 56th Street. My friendship with the Bonis has been one of the most rewarding and enduring of my life. Nell's kitchen had a profound effect on me. She and Albert became and have remained my "spiritual parents."

Nell's kitchen was the first truly thoughtful kitchen I'd ever seen, impressive not only for its collection of antique copper (which she didn't use for cooking) and pewter, but also for the handsome jars in which she stored her staples, the lovely bowls in which she mixed things. It wasn't at all like the antiseptic kitchen at home, with everything hidden from view. Nell was proud of hers, and she had a right to be.

Styles have changed since 1944. Cooks are no longer reluctant to display their equipment. The better the equipment, the easier the task. The handsomer it is, the more pleasant it is to work with. I'm obviously speaking in defense of kitchens that are not merely well planned, but well decorated. It is probably the most important room in the house—despite the popular European conviction that Americans must live in their bathrooms, since each house has so many of them.

WHERE TO BUY IT IN NEW YORK

>Bazar de la Cuisine, 160 East 55th Street
Bazar Français, 666 Sixth Avenue
The Bridge Company, 212 East 52nd Street
Bonnier, Inc., 605 Madison Avenue
La Cuisinière, Inc., 903 Madison Avenue
Hammacher Schlemmer, 147 East 57th Street
The Pottery Barn, 227 East 60th Street, 231 Tenth Avenue

WHAT TO BUY

>This is *not* a complete list of kitchen equipment. Your needs will depend on the size of your household, your taste in cooking, and the amount of space (and money) you can spare. As I've noted in the body of the text, bargains in cookware are more often false economies than good buys. But if you travel in Europe, visit some of the department stores or specialty shops to find some of the more exotic items.

>*Baking pans:* Two or three round ones, 8 inches in diameter, or the same number of square pans, 8 inches to a side, depending on the shape of cake you like to make.

>>Rectangular pans for brownies and special cakes.
Spring cake pans, for many European cakes and tortes. They spring loose to facilitate the removal of the cake.
Angel food pan.
Kugelhof pan.
Two-cup cake pans.
At least 2 miniature cupcake pans, ideal for making small *quiches.*

Bulb syringe baster.
Electric blender.

Brushes:
   Pastry brush.
   Brush for applying barbecue sauce.
   Vegetable brush.
   Pot brush.

Cake cover: Invaluable if you bake cakes frequently. If not, a large bowl turned upside down will do.

Cake pans (see *Baking pans*).

Cake racks.

Cake tester.

Casseroles: The quantities and sizes and materials will depend on your needs. They are available in Pyrex, enameled cast iron, ceramic, and copper. The enameled cast iron is the best all-around ware.

Cheesecloth: It has many kitchen applications.

Chopping board: Should be heavy wood, or butcher block, and be capable of sustaining the blows of a large knife.

Chopping bowl and chopper: For some jobs, there is no substitute. Ideally, you should have large and small bowls and choppers.

Cleaver: Not a necessity, but an occasional convenience.

Cocottes: Available in many materials and sizes. Mine are copper, earthenware, and enameled cast iron. As for casseroles, I recommend the last.

Coffeepot: The best and most economical coffeemaker is a French ceramic drip coffeepot. Because of its material, it can be completely freed of all persistent coffee oils that make for bitterness.

Colander: I suggest you buy two, one of regular size in enameled steel, and a larger aluminum colander for draining such foods as spaghetti.

Cookie sheets: At least two. The ones with Teflon coating are wonderful; nothing sticks to them.

Cooking stones: Friends and relations tease me about my passion for stones, but they are useful as well as beautiful, especially round or oblong ones for use as weights, for grinding bread crumbs, and for cracking lobster shells.

Custard cups.
Deep fryer with removable basket.
Double boiler: You need a large one (1- or 2-quart capacity) for general use, and a smaller one, designed for heating baby food, which is ideal for making hollandaise and *béarnaise* and small quantities of cream sauce.
Dutch oven: Cast iron is the only kind.
Egg beater: Electrically operated, if possible.
Exhaust fan: You can't do without one for long if you do a lot of deep frying.
Feather brush: For basting legs and wings of fowl.
Flame-tamers: The flame-tamer consists of two layers of metal, sometimes perforated, sometimes slotted, that reduces the level of heat emitted by a gas burner far more than even the simmer level does. It makes it possible for you to place oven china on the stove with safety, and occasionally will make it unnecessary to make use of a double boiler.
Flour sifter.
Food mill: It is preferable to have two, a small one for little jobs, and the larger for such things as mashed potatoes and large quantities of purée.
French beaner: A gadget for "Frenching" beans, i.e., making three or four longitudinal slices.
Graters: The "Mouli," made in France, is the best for all-around purposes, notably for vegetables and cheese. Mouli makes several models. They should be discarded when they become dull—which is difficult; one develops an attachment to them.
Gratin dishes: These come in oval and circular shapes and in several materials, including glass. I prefer enameled cast iron.
Carving knife: If you have someone in your house who knows how to keep a knife sharp, the carbon-steel variety will take a much better edge than one of stainless steel. The former rusts if you don't keep it dry, but it works better.

Knife sharpener: To have in place of a person—a poor but adequate substitute for an expert.

Knives: I feel about knives in general as I feel about a carving knife—preferring the carbon-steel to the stainless kinds. There are some exceptions: tomato, bread, and citrus knives are always stainless, with serrated edges that don't require sharpening. However, the balance of your selection should be the traditional sort. They should range from the smallest paring knife to the largest chopping knife. One never has too many good knives.

Ladles: At least two, large and small, for soups, sauces, and other runny things.

Larding needles (see p. 73).

Lemon squeezer: The best for normal cooking purposes is the old-fashioned kind which requires that you twist half a lemon down on it.

Linen cloths: These can be dish towels. I use them in cooking, however, for dampening and covering sandwiches, rolling a jelly roll, or keeping cold turkey moist. For dish toweling, I use terry cloth (see below).

Marinating pot: Almost any container will do, provided it holds the piece to be marinated snugly. I use enameled cast iron.

Measuring cups: I have a set that allows me to level the ingredients without spilling them. The Pyrex pint and quart measures are generally helpful for more than just measuring.

Measuring spoons.

Meat grinder: The large old-fashioned, hand-cranked models are still around and they still work. Get an electric model, if you're able—they often are available with your mixer.

Meat trivet: A must for propping up roasts of meat and fowl in the oven.

Electric mixers: If your spouse or good friend would like to make you an important gift, ask for a Braun or Hobart Kitchen Machine. It does everything: mixing, grinding, chopping, puréeing, slicing, and even dough kneading.

It will set you back a bundle, but it is built like a Rolls Royce and should last as long as your own teeth do. I am fortunate to have a hand electric mixer as well; in cakemaking I use both.

Mixing bowls: You'll need many. I have a couple of nests, but I really prefer a collection of ones ideal for each purpose.

Molds: These are generally of copper or aluminum, and useful, but not essential. If the design is pretty or amusing, it can add something to a jellied dish.

Muslin: For straining soups and jelly. You should have a few yards of the unbleached kind on hand. Be sure to wash it before you use it, or the sizing in the material will add an unexpected starch to your dish.

Omelet pan: One with a Teflon surface is ideal.

Openers: Despite my being indulged with a Braun Kitchen Machine, I find something decadent in electric can openers. The hand variety is not much work, and one thus does one's bit for fuel conservation.

Squeezers: For oranges, lemons, garlic, etc. You should have the number you need. For oranges, the cast-aluminum model presses the fruit and extracts the greatest quantity of juice.

Pancake turners: One small, one large, of stainless steel.

Pastry blender: Useful if you won't use your bare hands or don't trust them.

Peelers: The plain ones are a necessity. The fancy ones create little wonders with citrus rinds, etc. They must be sharp.

Pepper mills: Indispensable, in at least two sizes—a big one for the stove, a small one for the table.

Pie plates, tart tins: Your tendency to bake will determine your needs. I prefer china or Pyrex to the metal ones.

Roasting fork.

Roasting pan: Must be large enough to hold a trivet, and have a lid for braising.

Roasting thermometer.
Rolling pin.
Saucepans: You should have as many sizes as you can afford and store, ranging in size from a dollhouse set to the largest. If I hadn't been collecting copper saucepans for most of my adult life, I would buy enameled cast iron. I would avoid most aluminum pans, except those that are not flimsy. The stainless steel ones with copper bottoms are satisfactory, provided they are of the heaviest weight.
Sautéing pans: Several sizes are desirable. In a pinch, a cast-iron frying pan will do.
Scales: If they are reliable, they are very useful for all sorts of cooking purposes—especially if you use English cookbooks, which are based on the metric system.
Scissors: Two pairs—a large one for gross kitchen purposes, and a pair of nail scissors for trimming things like shrimp.
Sieves: You need at least three sizes, ranging from the variety used to strain tea to the largest. The best ones are of stainless steel, usually to be obtained from restaurant supply companies.
Skewers: You need a variety of sizes for different purposes.
Skillets: For all-around use, nothing surpasses the heavy cast-iron wear. You should have at least two, preferably four sizes.
Skimmer (see p. 64).
Soufflé dishes: In Pyrex or ceramic, these are very useful for making custards as well.
Soup pot or marmite: The bigger the better. Copper or ceramic are best, but you have to cure the latter before use, and it is fragile. The hotel stainless steel models are also good.
Spatulas: You should accumulate a collection of shapes, sizes, and materials. You need at least two of the rubber ones. I can't think how we ever managed without them. You should also have one metal or wooden spatula for such tasks as loosening cakes and applying icings.

Perforated metal spoon.

Spoons: I feel as if I could write an entire volume of short essays on each of my wooden spoons. I must have twenty that differ from each other—some with holes in the center, others slotted, blunt-ended, scoop-shaped, shovel-shaped. I never think I have enough. But I guess I really do. Don't forget a very little one for starting mayonnaise, and a wooden fork and spoon set for serving salad.

Steamers: There are two types, and you'll probably need both—one that stands on legs for steaming small amounts, and a larger one for foods like potatoes.

Storage containers: These should be in a variety of sizes and materials, depending on purpose.

Terry cloth dish towels: I've been using them for years. I don't understand why one should use anything else.

Deep fat thermometer: Will also measure the temperature of sugar, a must for frying and preparing icings.

Tongs: They come in wood and metal, in many shapes and sizes—all useful.

Wire whisks: At least two—small and medium—are essential.

APPENDIX III

An Opinionated Bibliography

Due notice should be taken that this is not merely a selected bibliography; it is opinionated. The list below comprehends the cookbooks that I admire most, for one reason or another. It is neither exhaustive nor deliberately representative of all styles or nationalities of cooking.

American Cookery, James Beard. Little, Brown, 1942. No one has ever written a better, more interesting, or more comprehensive guide to our national styles of cooking.

The Art of Eating, M. F. K. Fisher. Macmillan, 1954. This is more interesting for her philosophy of cooking than for her recipes.

The Art of French Cooking. Simon & Schuster, 1958. This is one of those fat French works, a committee production, that contains much useful information.

The Chinese Cookbook, Wallace Yee Hong. Crown, 1952. As a novice in Oriental cooking, I swear by this book.

Clementine in the Kitchen, Phineas Beck (Samuel Chamberlain). Hastings House, 1942. A gem. One of the first books concerned with food in all its aspects. I have read it from cover to cover many times. I still treasure many of the recipes. Ideal for those who love France and her food.

Cooking à la Ritz, Louis Diat. Lippincott, 1941. Worth the price just for the recipe for lamb stew and the recipes for serving cold meats.

La Cuisine, Raymond Oliver. Bordas (Paris), 1965. A volume devoted to the "new style" of French cooking by the man who has become France's Julia Child. An edition in English is available.

La Cuisine de France, Mapie, Countess de Toulouse-Lautrec. Orion Press, 1964. A modern French cookbook, well worth having, and often easy on the purse.

Escoffier Cookbook, A. Escoffier. Crown, 1941. This is a professional's cookbook. It contains all that needs to be written about French cooking and cooking in general. It is not easy to apply in the average home kitchen, but it is great for study. If you learn all that Maître Escoffier imparts, you'll be peerless.

French Cooking for Americans, Louis Diat. Lippincott, 1946. Essential for all who would learn "plain French cooking." It has been a favorite of mine since it was first published.

French Provincial Cooking, Elizabeth David. Harper & Row, 1962. All of Elizabeth David's books are now in paperback editions and worth buying. This, however, is her masterpiece. A most delightful and sensible work.

The Gentleman's Companion, Charles H. Baker. Crown, 1946. Spotty, but it contains some interesting reflections about food, and some good recipes for both food and drink.

The Gold Cook Book, Louis P. de Gouy. Greenberg, 1948. This would be my choice for the ideal big, "American," general cookbook. Especially fine on baking and pastry-making.

Gourmet Cookbooks, Vols. I and II. *Gourmet* Magazine, 1950 and 1957. An invaluable committee job, notable for quality and breadth of coverage.

An Opinionated Bibliography 215

The Great Book of French Cuisine, Henri-Paul Pellaprat. World, 1971. If one could have only one lavish work, this would be my choice. Filled with sound advice about *haute cuisine*.

Grossman's Guide to Wine, Spirits, and Beer. Scribner's, 1940 and 1964. A valuable work on a subject intimately related to food, its preparation and service.

James Beard's Fish Cookery. Little, Brown, 1954. One of the best books available on this specialized theme.

June Platt Cook Book. Knopf, 1958. This is a condensation of June Platt's earlier books, all of which are long out of print. This, too, is out of print, but you just might find a copy. If you do, pay any reasonable price for it. She's tops.

The Kitchen Scholar, Malvina C. Kinard and Marjorie P. Blanchard. Citadel Press, 1967. Lots of good hints, especially about soufflés.

Larousse Gastronomique. Crown, 1961. I haven't checked, but I suspect this enormous and indispensable compendium of encyclopedic intent and arrangement would tell you just a little more about any given aspect of cooking than you really want to know. But never less.

Mastering the Art of French Cooking, Vol. I, Simone Beck, Louisette Bertholle, and Julia Child. Knopf, 1961. Just what the title suggests. Some readers, experienced cooks, find the organization confusing. I wouldn't be without it.

Mastering the Art of French Cooking, Vol. II, Julia Child and Simone Beck. Knopf, 1970. As useful as its predecessor. Superb details on bread baking.

New York Guidebook: The Passionate Shopper, Elizabeth Lohman Scharlatt and the editors of *New York*. Dutton, 1972. Handy for all sorts of shops, notably food and spice suppliers for the happy cooker.

The New York Times Cookbook, Craig Claiborne. Harper & Row, 1961. The best of all "general" cookbooks. Should replace *The Joy of Cooking* and Fanny Farmer. Especially good for its organization of recipes and excellent information.

Nobody Ever Tells You These Things, Helen McCully. Holt, Rinehart and Winston, 1967. Helen McCully *does* tell you. The book is full of valuable information, usefully arranged.

Party Cook Book, June Platt. Houghton Mifflin, 1936. Even though it is out of print and would be worth its weight in gold if you found one, I couldn't be conscientious without including it. The book changed my life.

The Seasonal Kitchen, Perla Meyers. Holt, Rinehart and Winston, 1973. Dwells at length on a point I make often: that it is pleasant to follow a regime inspired by what is available seasonally. A new stimulant among the quantities of cookbooks now appearing.

Uniform Retail Meat Identity Standards, the National Livestock and Meat Board, 36 Wabash Avenue, Chicago, Illinois 60603. Price $6. The abundant amount of important information included in this book was brought to my attention too late for inclusion within the text of my own.

Wine, Hugh Johnson. Simon & Schuster, 1972. I think this one of the better wine books. It covers more than the French wines—and deals with *them* admirably.

Wines of France, Alexis Lichine. Knopf, 1951. This remains the basic book on French wine for Americans.

INDEX

Aging of meat, 7
À la poêle
  defined, 93
  en casserole, 94–95
  en cocotte, 94–95
  techniques of preparing, 93–94
Allspice, 146
Aluminum foil, roasting in, 15
Appetizers, selection and service of, 195
Artichoke(s)
  hearts, preparation of, 169
  Jerusalem, 174
  salvaging browned, 170
  service of, 168, 169
  whole, preparation of, 168–169
Art of Carving, The, 36
Asparagus, selection and preparation of, 170
Au gratin, 95

Baking, cake
  equipment for, 154–155
  ingredients for, 154–155
  techniques of, 155–158
Baking, cookies, 160
Baking, pastry
  equipment for, 158–159
  puff, 160
  techniques of, 159–160
Ballottine, 97
Barding
  defined, 17
  of fowl for roasting, 24
  of meat for roasting, 17
Basil, 145
Basting
  of broiled meats, 28
  need for in spit-roasting, 35
  of roasts, 19
Batter, techniques of deep frying foods in, 43
Bay (leaf), 145
Beans
  dried, 176–177
  green, 171
Beck, Simone, 153
Beef
  cuts suitable for boiling, 66

Beef (*continued*)
  cuts suitable for braising, 85
  cuts suitable for broiling, 26
  cuts suitable for fricasseeing, 92–93
  cuts suitable for pan frying, 48
  cuts suitable for pot roasting, 92
  cuts suitable for roasting, 16
  cuts suitable for sautéeing, 48
  cuts suitable for stewing, 68
  grading of, 10
  physical appearance of quality raw, 11
  standard cuts of, 8–9
  time table for broiling, 29–30
  time table for roasting, 21
Beets, 171
Beurre manié
  defined, 78, 80
  techniques of preparing, 80
  use of, 67
Binding agents, 106
Birds, stuffed, roasting of, 24
  see also Fowl
Bisque, 124–125
Blanching, 75
Boiling
  defined, 63–64
  equipment for, 64
  foods suitable for, 66
  techniques of, 64–65
Bologna, 98

Bones
  cooked, use in stockmaking, 58–59
  use in braising, 90–91
Boni, Albert, 205
Boni, Nell, 119, 205
Bouillon, 122–123
Bouquet garni, 146
Braider, Donald, 60, 61, 117–119
Braider, Susan, 151–152
Brains, poaching of, 71
Braising
  cuts of meat suitable for, 85–86
  defined, 84
  equipment for, 86
  of red meats, 88–89
  of specialty meats, 90
  techniques of, 89–90
  use of bones in, 90–91
  of "white" meats, 89–90
Breading, techniques of, 45–46
Breadmaking, 153
Broccoli, 171–172
Broiling
  cuts of meat suitable for, 26–27
  fish fillet and steak, techniques of, 31
  fowl, techniques of, 31
  kinds of seafood suitable for, 27
  lobster, techniques of, 32
  meat, techniques of, 27–32
  time tables for, 29–30

Brown stock, 52–53
Buffet dinners, 196–197
Bulk measures, 202
Butcher, cultivating a, 7
Butter
   clarified, preparation of, 45
   use in glazing, 95

Cabbage, 172
Cakes
   equipment for baking, 155
   ingredients for baking, 154–155
   spice, xiv–xviii
   techniques of baking, 155–158
Capers, 150
Capon, roasting of, 16, 24
   see also Fowl
Carrots, 172
Carter, Germaine, 194
Carving, techniques of, 36
Cayenne, 146
Celeriac, 172
Celery, 172
   root, 172
Chamberlain, Samuel, 194
Charcoal grill cookery, 33, 34
Chervil, 145
Chicken
   cuts suitable for fricasseeing, 93–94
   cuts suitable for roasting, 16
   physical appearance of quality raw, 12
   stock, 53
Chickpeas, 175–177
Child, Julia, 116, 153
Chives, 145
"Choice" grade of meat, 10
Chowder, 125
Cinnamon, 146
Clairborne, Craig, 182, 193
Clarified butter, preparation of, 45
Clarifying of stocks, 56–57
Clearness in meat, 10–13
Cloves, 146
Cocktails, service of, 197–198
Combination cooking
   à la poêle, 93–95
   au gratin, 95
   braising, 84–91
   defined, 82–83
   en casserole and *en cocotte*, 94–95
   fricasseeing, 92–93
   glazing, 95
   pot roasting, 91–92
Condiments, 150
Consommé, 122–123
Cookies, making, 160
Cooking
   combination, 82–95
   in liquids, 60–71
Corn, sweet, 173
Cornish game hen, roasting of, 24

Courses of a meal, how to select appropriate, 191–194, 197
Court bouillon, 57, 58
Crock of Gold, The, 198
Cucumbers, 173
Cured pork, time table for roasting, 22–23
Curry powder, 149
Custard, 114–115

David, Elizabeth, 56, 178, 193, 194
Deep frying
  equipment for, 39–40
  fats suitable for, 40
  techniques of, 41–43
  temperatures for, 42–43
  theory of, 38–39
De Gouy, Louis P., 153, 154
Dessert, selecting an appropriate, 192–193
Diat, Louis, 183, 184, 185, 193
Dill, 145
Dimyan, Edmund, 8
"Doneness," testing for
  with broiled food, 31
  with roasted food, 14–15
  with spit-roasted food, 35
Dried
  beans, 176–177
  peas, 176–177
Dry
  marinade, 74
  measures, metric, 203–204

Duck, techniques of cooking, 25
  see also Fowl
Dunn, Robert, 117–119

Egg(s)
  to add body and strength to foods, 106
  as binding agents, 106
  boiled, 109–110
  color of, 102
  as emulsifying agents, 106
  French-fried, 111
  fried, 110-111
  in glazing, 106
  grading of, 101
  how to break, 103
  as leavening agents, 106–107
  measures, 202
  oeufs mollet, 113
  omelets, 113–114
  peeling hard-boiled, 110
  poached, 112–113
  scrambled, 111–112
  shirred, 112
  sizes of, 101–102
  storage of, 102–103
  and temperature, 104
  used in clarifying stocks, 106
  versatility of, 100
  whites, beating of, 103–104, 107–108
Eggplant, 173–174
Electric rotisserie cookery, 33
Emulsifying agents, 106

En casserole, 94–95
En cocotte, 94–95
Endive, 174
Entrée, selection of, 192–193
Equipment, kitchen
    sources of supply, 206
    what to buy, 204–212
Escoffier, Maître, 142

Farmer, Fanny, 5
Fat, scoring of, 27
Fennel, 145, 174
Filets
    tenderness of, 6
    time table for roasting, 23
Fines herbes, 146
First cuts of meat, 6
Fish
    judging amount needed, 13
    kinds suitable for boiling, 66
    kinds suitable for panfrying, 48
    kinds suitable for sautéing, 48
    physical appearance of quality raw, 12–13
    stew, techniques of preparing, 69
    storing raw, 13
    techniques of broiling, 31–32
    techniques of poaching, 70–71
    techniques of roasting, 25–26
Fisher, M. F. K., 189

Flame, how to extinguish, 33
Flavorings, 142–150
Foil, aluminum, roasting in, 15
Folding, techniques of, 108–109
Forcemeats, 96–98
Fowl
    cuts suitable for boiling, 66
    cuts suitable for braising, 86
    cuts suitable for broiling, 27
    cuts suitable for panfrying, 48
    cuts suitable for poaching, 71
    cuts suitable for pot roasting, 92
    cuts suitable for roasting, 16–17
    cuts suitable for sautéing, 48
    cuts suitable for stewing, 68
    grease from, uses of, 25
    making stock from, 25
    physical appearance of quality raw, 12
    stuffed, roasting of, 24
    techniques of broiling, 31
    techniques of fricasseeing, 93
    techniques of poaching, 70–71
    techniques of roasting, 16–17, 23–24
    techniques of spit-roasting, 23, 25
    techniques of stewing, 67–68
French Cooking for Americans, 183

French Provincial Cooking, 56
Fricasseeing, 92–93
Friture de la Loire, 38
Fruit
    selecting fresh, 177–178
    using preserved, 178–179
Fumet, 58

Galantine, 97
Game
    cuts suitable for braising, 86
    cuts suitable for pot roasting, 92
    cuts suitable for stewing, 68
    hen, *see* Fowl
Garbure, 125
Garlic, 145
Gastronomical Me, The, 189
Ginger, 146
Glace de viande, 57
Glazing
    defined, 95
    techniques of, 95–96
Gold Cook Book, The, 153
"Good" grade of meat, 10
Goose, *see* Fowl
Gourmet, 183
Grains, 176–177
Grease from fowl, uses of, 95
Green beans, 170–171
Grinod de la Reynière, 142

Haddock, *see* Seafood *and* Fish

Hall, Alan, 189
Hall, Kenneth, 189, 190, 191
Ham, time table for broiling, 30
Hanging of meat, 7
High-heat roasting technique, 20
Herbs, 142–146
    bouquet garni, 146
    fines herbes, 146
    list and uses of basic, 144–146
    see also names of specific herbs
Honey, 150
Hors d'oeuvres, selection and service of, 195

Jerusalem artichokes, 174
Jones, Mary Carter, 52
June Platt Cook Book, 136
Juniper, 145

Kasha, 177
Kidneys, braising of, 90
Kitchen equipment
    sources of supply, 206
    what to buy, 204–212
Kitchen Scholar, The, 116
Kohlrabi, 174

Lamb
    cuts suitable for boiling, 66
    cuts suitable for braising, 85
    cuts suitable for broiling, 26

cuts suitable for panfrying, 48
cuts suitable for pot roasting, 92
cuts suitable for roasting, 16
cuts suitable for sautéing, 48
cuts suitable for stewing, 68
grading of, 10
physical appearance of quality raw, 11
stuffed shoulder of, recipe for, 183–184
time table for broiling, 30
time table for roasting, 21
Larding, 73
Leavening agents, 106–107
Leeks, 174
Leftovers, used in making stock, 58–59
Lemon, zest of, 147–148
Lentils, 176–177
Liebling, A. J., 163
Liquid
  custard, 114
  marinade, 74
  measures, tables of, 201, 204
Lobster
  bisque, preparation of, 118–119
  how to pulverize shells of, 119
  techniques of boiling, 60–61
  techniques of broiling, 31–32
  see also Seafood *and* Fish
Low-heat roasting technique, 20

Mace, 147
Madeira, 77
Main courses, selecting appropriate, 192–193
Mapie, Countess de Toulouse-Lautrec, 23
"Marbling" in meat, 6
Margarine
  unsuitability as basting medium, 31
  unsuitability in deep frying, 44
Marinades, liquid and dry, 74
Marinating
  defined, 73–74
  equipment for, 74
  techniques of, 74–75
Marjoram, 145
Mastering the Art of French Cooking, 153, 182
Matignon, 77
Mayonnaise, 134–136
Measures
  tables of, 201–203
    American versus British, 201–202
    American versus metric, 203–204
    bulk, 202
    dry, 203
    egg, 202
    liquid, 201, 204
    odd, 202
    temperature, 201

Meat
  aging of, 7
  boiled, pressing of, 65
  calculating amount needed for roasting, 13
  clearness of, 10–13
  first cuts of, 6
  glazing, 96
  grades of, 10
  hanging of, 7
  packaging of, 11
  physical appearance of quality raw, 10–13
  searing of, 27
  standard cuts of, 8–9
  stew, techniques of preparing, 67–69
  thermometer, need for in roasting, 14
  see also names of specific kinds of meats
Meat loaf, 96–98
Menus
  planning, 188–194
  sample, 193–194
  variety desirable in, 192
Metric measures, table of, 203–204
Minestrone, 125
Mint, 145
Mirepoix, 76–77
Mistakes in cooking, how to deal with, 186–187
Monosodium glutamate, 149
Moody, Mrs., 5
Morgan, J. P., 153

Mousses, 115–116
M.S.G., 149
Mushrooms, 174–175
Mustard, 147, 150

National Live Stock and Meat Board, 9
New York Times Cookbook, The, 182
Nutmeg, 147

Oeufs mollet, 113
Omelets, 113–114
Onions, 175
Orange, zest of, 147–148
Oregano, 145
Oven thermometer, reliability of, 18–19

Packaging of meat, 11
Panbroiling, techniques of, 32–33
Panfrying
  contrasted with sautéing, 44
  equipment for, 46
  fats suitable for, 44
  foods suitable for, 48
  techniques of, 46–47
  theory of, 43
Paprika, 147
Parisian spice, 148
Parsley, 145
Party Cook Book, 5, 189

Index

Pasta, 176–177
Pastry
  cake baking, 154–157
  cookie baking, 160
  equipment for making, 158–159
  puff, 160
  techniques of making, 159–160
Pâté, 96–98
  en croute, 97
Pâtisserie, 152
Peas, dried, 176–177
Pepper, black and white, 147, 149
Petite marmite, 123
Pheasant, techniques of cooking, 25
  see also Fowl
Pickles, 150
Planning
  cooking time, 184–185
  menus, 188–194
  seating arrangements, 196
Platt, June, 5, 111, 189, 193, 194
Poaching, 70–71
Pork
  chops, Dutch-oven, 33
  cured, time table for roasting, 22–23
  cuts suitable for braising, 86
  cuts suitable for broiling, 27
  cuts suitable for panfrying, 48

cuts suitable for pot roasting, 92
cuts suitable for roasting, 16
cuts suitable for sautéing, 48
cuts suitable for spit-roasting, 35
grading of, 10
physical appearance of quality raw, 12
time table for broiling, 30
time table for roasting, 22
Potage Henri IV, 123
Potatoes, 175
Pot au feu, 52, 123
Pot roasting, 92
Preparation time, as factor in menu planning, 197
"Prime" grade of meat, 10
Pudding, 114–115
Puff pastry, 160
Pungents, 150
Purée, 123–124

Quatre épices, 148
Quenelles, 115–116
Quiches, 114–115

Recipes
  how to approach, 181–182
  how to read, 182–187
Reducing of stocks, 57
Rendering, techniques of, 40–41
"Resting" roasts, 20

Rib roast, standing
　how to prepare, 14, 19
　proper size of, 17–18
Rice, 176–177
Rissole, 176–177
Roasting
　bags, 15
　cooking time, how to
　　calculate, 20–23
　cuts of meat and fish
　　suitable for, 16–17
　fish, techniques of, 25–26
　meat, techniques of, 18–20
　proper shape of meat for, 18
　proper size of meat for,
　　17–18
　standing ribs, 14
　temperatures for, 18–20
　testing for "doneness," 4–15
　theories of, 19–20
　time tables for, 21–22
Rogers, Dorothy, 52
Rosemary, 145
Rotisserie, electric,
　spit-roasting on a, 33
Roux, 67
　equipment for preparing, 79
　storage of, 80
　techniques of preparing,
　　79–80
　types of, 78

Saffron, 147
Sage, 145
Salami, 98

Salmon, *see* Seafood *and* Fish
Salt(s), 142–144
　kinds of, 148–149
Sauce(s)
　basic types of, 128–129,
　　132–141
　béarnaise, 134, 137
　béchamel, 133–134
　bordelaise, 141
　bourguignonne, 132–133
　brown, 132
　compound, 139–140
　egg, 134–137
　equipment for preparing,
　　131
　espagnole, recipe for,
　　140–141
　hollandaise, 134, 136–137
　mayonnaise, 135–136
　paloise, 137–138
　preparing contrasting,
　　130–131
　preparing homogeneous,
　　129–130
　tomato, 138–139
　velouté, 133
　vinaigrette, 139
　white, 133–134
Sausage, 96–98
Sautéing
　contrasted with frying, 44
　equipment for, 46
　foods suitable for, 48
　as preliminary step in
　　combination cooking,
　　44

as preliminary step in
    saucemaking, 47–48
techniques of, 46–47
theory of, 43–44
Seafood
    kinds suitable for boiling, 66
    kinds suitable for broiling, 27
    see also names of specific
        kinds of seafood
Seasonings, hot, 149
Seating arrangements, 196
Serving suggestions, 195–196
Soufflés, 115–116
Soup
    equipment for making, 122
    freezing of, 121
    serving of, 120–121
    types of, 122–126
Spice(s)
    cake, making a, xiv–xviii
    list and uses of basic,
        146–148
    quatre épices, 148
    see also names of specific
        spices
Spit-roasting, 33–35
    cuts of meat suitable for,
        35
    fire suitable for, 34
    pros and cons of, 35
    techniques of, 34–35
    timing of, 35
Squab, see Fowl
Standing rib roast
    preparation of a, 14, 19
    proper size of, 17–18

Starches, 176–177
Steaming, 62–63
Stephens, James, 198
Stew(s)
    fish, 69
    meat, techniques of
        preparing, 67–69
    seasoning of, 67
Stewing
    defined, 66
    foods suitable for, 68
    techniques of preparing a
        meat stew, 67–69
    time required for, 68
Stock
    brown, 52–53
    as by-product of liquid
        cooking, 62
    chicken, 53
    clarifying, 56–57
    court bouillon, 57, 58
    defined, 49–50
    equipment for making,
        54–55
    fumet, 58
    glace de viande, 57
    homemade versus canned,
        51–52
    made from roast fowl, 25
    made from leftovers, 58–59
    meager, 58–59
    preparation of, 49–50, 55
    preserving, 52
    reducing, 57
    straining, 55–56
    types of, 52–54

Stock (*continued*)
  uses of, 51–52
  white, 54
Stuffed birds, roasting of, 24
Sugar, 150
Sweetbreads
  braising of, 90
  poaching of, 71
Sweet corn, 173
Sweeteners, 142–144, 150
Swordfish, *see* Seafood *and* Fish

Tarragon, 146
Temperature
  measures of, 201
  for roasting, 19–20
Terrine, 97
Thermometer
  meat, need for in roasting, 14
  oven, 18–19
  sugar syrup, 39
Thermostat, broiler, reliability of, 26
Thickening agents, 106
Thick-sauce glazing, 96
"Thinking through" a recipe, 180–187
Thyme, 146
Time tables
  for broiling meats, 29–30
  for roasting meats and fowl, 21–22
Tomatoes, 175–176

Tongue, braising of, 90
Turkey
  physical appearance of quality raw, 12
  techniques of broiling young, 31
  techniques of roasting, 16–17, 24
  see also Fowl

Vanilla, 147
Veal
  cuts suitable for boiling, 66
  cuts suitable for braising, 86
  cuts suitable for broiling, 26–27
  cuts suitable for fricasseeing, 92–93
  cuts suitable for panfrying, 48
  cuts suitable for pot roasting, 92
  cuts suitable for roasting, 16
  cuts suitable for sautéing, 48
  cuts suitable for stewing, 68
  grading of, 10
  physical appearance of quality raw, 11–12
  time table for roasting, 22
Vegetables
  boiling of, 66, 166
  choosing fresh, frozen, or canned, 162–163
  cooking dried, 167–168
  cooking fresh, 166–167

cooking frozen, 167
growing, 162
judging fresh, 165
panfrying of, 48
preparing fresh, 165–166
sautéing of, 48
steaming of, 168
see also names of specific vegetables
Velouté, 124–125, 133
Verdery, John, 36

da Vinci, Leonardo, 99
Vinegar, 149

Weights, tables of, 203–204
"White" meat
  broiling of, 28
  spit-roasting of, 34–35
White stock, 54
Wood embers, spit-roasting over, 34